RESEARCH ETHICS, INDIGENOUS COMMUNITIES AND FIELDWORK

RESEARCH ETHICS, INDIGENOUS COMMUNITIES AND FIELDWORK

Edited by
SUBIR BISWAS

RESEARCH INDIA PRESS
New Delhi (INDIA)

Research Ethics, Indigenous Communities and Fieldwork

© **Editor**

ISBN : 978-93-5171-023-3

First Edition: 2021

All right reserved. No part of this publication may be reproduced in any form without the prior written permission of the Authors.

Published by :
RESEARCH INDIA PRESS
E-6/34, Sangam Vihar
New Delhi-110062
Phone: 011-26047013, (M) 9818085794
E-mail: researchindiapress@gmail.com

Type Setting & Design by
G. R. Sharma

Contents

Preface		*vii*
List of Contributors		*xiii*

1. Empirical Research Ethics: An Overview with Special Reference to India
   Subhamay Kisku — 1

2. Ethical Issues Relating to Fieldwork among Indigenous Communities
   Rajat Kanti Das — 14

3. Ethical Issues for doing Fieldwork among Indigenous People of India
   K K Ganguly — 25

4. Issues and Challenges in Conducting Ethnographic Research among Indigenous Communities in Bihar and Jharkhand
   Rajeev Kamal Kumar — 33

5. Ethical Issues with Indigenous and Non-Indigenous Populations: Some Considerations
   Gautam Kumar Kshatriya — 60

6. Ethical Issues in Anthropology: Focusing Qualitative Research, Reflexive Method and Field Work
   Sekh Rahim Mondal — 75

7. Ethical Issues in Fieldwork: Traditional versus Modern Approach   87
   Monika Saini and A. K. Kapoor

8. Ethical issues in Anthropological Research: Participant Observation   98
   Subir Biswas

9. GREATS - Guidelines for Research Ethics in Anthropological Studies: An Appraisal   107
   Mithun Das

Preface

To enact area or population wise ethical issues for doing research/ fieldwork for anthropology professionals and students are essential because of its complex nature and cultural relativism. Fieldwork among indigenous population is not only difficult in nature but need to understand their culture before going to or conducting fieldwork among them. It is well known fact that the code enacted by western or even neighboring countries may not suit for Indian perspectives; even fieldwork among different Indigenous population from different part of India needs different types of intervention for doing fieldwork. These are the reasons why we need non-procedural ethics to interact; however present-day research also demands lots of procedural ethics for doing anthropological research/ fieldwork.

On the other hand, Anthropology, because of its uniqueness, requires different types of ethical considerations during fieldwork. Social-Cultural Anthropology requires consent from individuals or even community; whereas Biological Anthropologist requires more attention on physical harm because of specific techniques. Similarly, Archaeologist requires community consent besides the adherence to the governmental rules and regulations.

Whatever it is, almost all western countries or even many eastern countries also enacted their own code of ethics for Anthropology professionals and students. However, in India, even after 100 years of institutional teaching of Anthropology we fail to understand it's importance and therefore there is no such code enacted by the Government bodies (except ICMR guidelines) or even by any associations of professional anthropologists.

Therefore, present book which is the byproduct of ICSSR IMPREESS supported workshop, will help policy makers like Government agencies and professional anthropological associations to enact formal ethical code for doing field work among Indian population.

The present volume is a compilation of nine articles related with ethical issues during research/ fieldwork in general and more specifically among indigenous communities.

In first article, "Empirical Research Ethics: An Overview with Special Reference to India", Subhamay Kisku after assessing ethical theories and principles documented his view on realities and prospects in empirical research specially among indigenous people of India. Rajat Kanti Das, in his article "Ethical issues relating to Fieldwork among Indigenous communities" has identified several checklists which supposed to be follow by the researcher during his/her fieldwork among said communities. KK Ganguly in his article "Ethical Issues for doing fieldwork among Indigenous People of India" very precisely opined about why Indian scenario needs for specific IRB for indigenous people's research. Rajeev Kamal Kumar in his paper "Issues and challenges in conducting Ethnographic research among Indigenous communities in Bihar and Jharkhand" nicely examined ethics as a methodological concern during his ethnographic study on Parhaiya, Tharu and Oraon communities. Gautam Kumar Kshatriya's article "Ethical issues with indigenous and non-indigenous populations: Some considerations" highlighting genetic and

IPs research on Havasupai and Yanomami communities as well as unethical drug trials affecting Indian communities. Sekh Rahim Mondal in his article "Issues in anthropology: Focusing qualitative research, reflexive method and Field work" nicely encounter with ethics and reflexibility in qualitative research specially in field condition. Monika Saini and A. K. Kapoor in "Ethical issues in Fieldwork: Traditional versus modern approach" logically identified ethical issues related with traditional and modern approaches of fieldwork specially from anthologist's perspectives. Subir Biswas in "Ethical issues in anthropological research: Participant observation" highlighted different ethical protocol to be obeyed during participant observation like- inform consent, IRB approval, maintaining privacy and confidentiality and so on. Mithun Das in his article "GREATS - Guidelines for research ethics in anthropological studies: An appraisal" after evaluating different international codes of ethics formulated his own guidelines specially for anthropological research in Indian context.

Beside their contribution in the form of articles, all the authors categorically recommended following issues to be incorporated when anthropological research to be conducted specially among indigenous communities in Indian context.

1. IEC process should be simple; follow up activities should be monitored by IEC extensively.

2. If possible, separate IEC may be established for ethnographic or Indigenous population research. We may think incorporation of members from indigenous communities as well to understand their perspectives.

3. Where the informants are non-literate the researcher can use recorded consent also depending on gravity of the consent.

4. Research proposal involving Indigenous people should be formulated after pilot survey where prior permission may be obtained from the participants/ research partners/ village headman.

5. Respect and recognition of Indigenous culture should be obeyed; and responsibilities, mindfulness and mutual benefits may be enhanced.

6. Authorship may be given to research partner depending on his/her contribution or researcher may acknowledge the name of important key informants beside the community; however, in all cases report should be accessible for research partners.

7. Purpose of academic research is different for different level of study like Undergraduate and Post graduate levels, which is mainly sensitization, orientation and training in nature; and such research/ study should conduct among nearby communities who are less vulnerable. The protocol of these studies may be cleared by departmental board instead of IEC. A simple guideline may be developed by the respective departments/University for the purpose of undergraduate and post graduate level field work. M. Phil and Ph.D. studies are as good as research where all IEC protocol should be obeyed.

8. Ethics for photography should be maintained strictly, including the field situation, individual space, consent for photographs, blocking the face of respondents may also be considered by the study team (situational based on the study topic, area and community).

9. Random sampling in such research is a delicate issue where families who are excluded sometimes may not

happy with several reasons. The issue may be taken care of positively during the field.

10. If you are collecting tools/ artifacts/ other such materials, please inform the community or you can organize an exhibition of the same.

11. Ethics should be included in Anthropology curriculum of all stages of study. Sensitization workshops for faculty/ scholars/ students are very much needed.

12. If you have new idea/ objectives after collection/ publication of data, please go back to the community/ participants for fresh consent.

List of Contributors

Dr. Subhamay Kisku, Assistant Professor, Department of Anthropology, University of Calcutta, 35, Ballygunge Circular Rd, Kolkata-700019, *E-mail: uksikyamahbus@ gmail.com*

Prof. Rajat Kanti Das, Former Professor, Department of Anthropology, Vidyasagar University, Midnapore, West Bengal 721102, *E-mail: rajat_p_das@yahoo.com*

Dr. KK Ganguly, Scientist-G, Indian Council of Medical Research, V. Ramalingaswami Bhawan Ansari Nagar, New Delhi – 110029, *E-mail: kalyanganguly@hotmail.com*

Dr. Rajeev Kamal Kumar, Assistant Professor in Sociology & Social Anthropology, A. N. Sinha Institute of Social Studies, Patna (Bihar), *E-mail: rkamalanthro@gmail.com*

Prof. Gautam Kshatriya, Former Professor, Department of Anthropology, University of Delhi, Delhi-110007, *E-mail: g26_51@yahoo.co.in*

Prof. Sekh Rahim Mondal, Former C C Sanyal Chair Professor of Anthropology and Sociology and Director, Centre for Himalayan Studies & Founder Head , Department of Anthropology, University of North Bengal, Raja Rammohunpur, Dist- Darjeeling-734013, *E-mail: rahimanthnbu@yahoo.co.in*

Prof. A. K. Kapoor, Former Vice-Chancellor, Jiwaji University, Gwalior, M.P. & former Professor, Department of Anthropology, University of Delhi, Delhi-110007, *E-mail: anupkapoor46@rediffmail.com*

Dr. Monika Saini, Assistant Professor, Department of Social Sciences, The National Institute of Health and Family Welfare, New Delhi-110067, *E-mail: drmonika@nihfw. org*

Prof. Subir Biswas, Professor of Anthropology, West Bengal State University, Barasat, Kolkata-700126, *E-mail: gargisubir@gmail.com*

Dr. Mithun Das, Associate Professor, Department of Anthropology, Sidho-Kanho-Birsha University, University Campus Road, Ranchi - Purulia Rd, Purulia, West Bengal 723104, *E-mail: mithundas01@yahoo.com*

CHAPTER – 1

Empirical Research Ethics: An Overview with Special Reference to India

SUBHAMAY KISKU

Ethics

There is no such universal law between what is right and what is wrong. The concept of right and wrong vary a lot. According to Herodotus, there are little more than what is 'right' and 'wrong' in the social convention (Mensch 2014). For example, headhunting has been practised among the Mizo and the Naga ethnic groups till the 19th century (Zou, 2005). It was a custom that was perceived as cultural right by those ethnic groups. So, we can't say that any custom is 'wrong', there are many people who think custom appease evil spirit and also pride for them. But, if one particular behaviour is preferred in one society, that does not mean that it is also preferred to all other societies. However, some behaviours are socially sanctioned and prescribed to perform across all societies. So, socially sanctioned behaviours are relative. These socially sanctioned behaviours are governed by some moral principles which are structured within the society and practice through culture. According to Plato, 'right' things are equivalent to the 'gods command', which is also known as the 'divine command' (Plato 2015). It is also true that moral principles are also guided by an individual's rationale and thinking process. Ethics is considered a moral philosophy (Blocker 1999). However, Socrates did not believe that the right things do not always relate to the appeasement of God (Rachels and Rachels 2007). Ethics is a subject matter of Philosophy. According to the Oxford dictionary, ethics is the study of what is right and wrong in human behaviours. It is also a belief about what is morally correct or acceptable (Mitra and Mitra 2015). So, human behaviours are ethically correct when those behaviours are morally also correct or acceptable. Though there are some exceptions and deviations, individual ethics are governed by a prescribed high standard of behaviours that are considered as good and right by most people in a society. Not only that it helps us to differentiate between ethical and unethical behaviours.

Human beings are free to do whatever they want to do. However, under the belief in determinism, this free will is denied. Determinists believe that all events are happened because of past events and with the proper knowledge one could predict these events (Gould 1998). Generally, human acts or behaves in a practical situation what she/ he thinks is right in that particular situation. For example, if a situation demands telling lies (saves one's life) and it is beneficial to the situation, then it is called the ethically correct decision. Though telling lies is not socially sanctioned behaviour in our society. There are some moral theories, which try to explain what ought to be done and why. These theories are as mentioned below (Tannsjo 2002).

1. Utilitarianism
2. Egoism
3. Deontological Ethics
4. The Ethics of Rights

5. Virtue Ethics
6. Feminist Ethics
7. Environmental or Ecological Ethics

Ethical Relativism

According to Kant "Act only according to that maxim by which you can at the same time will that it should become a universal law" (Semple 1871). He called it the ultimate moral principle, the 'Categorical Imperative'. It says that certain principles are to be followed (maxim) to perform an act if these principles are followed by everyone (universal law) then the act is permissible. There are no universally accepted cross-cultural, normative ethical standards – it is all culturally relative. As mentioned earlier, there are no such ethical standards which equally accepted throughout societies and culturally. Each culture has its ethical standards. It is guided by numerous cultural sources, like norms, values, beliefs, customs, and morals. For individuals, the sources may be determined by multiple cultural components, socialization process, experiences towards social facts, and psychological development. Apart from these, they may be religious, political ideologies, or pragmatic observations of what seems to work and what doesn't. Social and cultural ethics vary in different societies and cultures. Say for example homosexuality is a natural phenomenon. However, some of the countries look at it as abnormal behaviour whereas many countries look at it as natural, so they have given same-sex marriage a legal sanction.

Ethical Principles in Research

With the development of science and technology, we have been experiencing enumerable opportunities in our daily life. But at the same time, we have been experiencing some ethical considerations in the sphere of the health care services. Technically this consideration is known as bioethics. To define the concept of bioethics, it is considered as the study of ethical questions that relate to the life and biological well-being of people (DeVries and Subedi, 1998). Issues that come under bioethical consideration like a prolongation of life and distribution of limited health care resources (Sullivan 2000). Some other issues are in dilemma like abortion, cloning, euthanasia, assisted suicide, and so on.

In bioethics, the most accepted principles are individual autonomy, beneficence, non-maleficence, and justice (World Health Organization 2009). It is a basic responsibility of a researcher to think all beneficence for each participant in the research activity. The success of any research primarily depends upon the research participants. So, it is a liability of the researcher to make sure for providing all the justified things to the research participants. Sometimes, research participants have to face difficulties or odds for participating in a research program, in that case, it is the sole liability of a researcher to protect the participants. If it is known to a researcher that there is an inadvertent worse effect on the participants due to the participation in the research activity, then the researcher must try to avoid that oddness. If not possible to avoid them it must be explained well in advance to the participants, in that case, the researcher must respect the wishes of the participants if she or he wants to withdraw from the research. So, it is a liability of the researcher to respect the autonomy of the research participant. In another way, a researcher has a huge responsibility for the well-being of the research participants. Safety must be a prime concern in any research activity. Whether the research participants are human or non-human it does not matter it comes under the purview of the research ethics the all the safety measures are taken care of in the research program. Not only that it must be ensured that all research participants take part in research with self-dignity. Here, comes the role of a researcher to interact with the participants in a dignified manner and also allow others to interact with the participants in a dignified way.

Ethics in Social Science Research

Social science research is a kind of research in which issues related to human societies are studied. So, it is obvious that human beings are considered as the main concern in social science research. Here comes again ethical concern related to the human being. In the case of social science research ethical concern is a little different from the rest of the other researches in different non-social science research especially in biological science. In social science research, both researcher and research participants are human beings and they are entitled to enjoy equal rights, there is some added responsibility on the researcher to maintain certain research ethics. First, participation in social science research will be voluntary. If possible, written consent or declaration may be kept before the participation. In the case of a non-literate participant, the help of the participant's trustworthy literate person may be pursued. Until then she or he should not be involved in the research. If these are not possible in all the cases, at least verbal consent may be taken. So, if require, participants will be in a position to answer that they are well aware of the research objectives and understanding that they voluntarily join in the research activity as a participant. Above all safety and security of the participants is a prime concern that has to be understood in all respect. Only avoidance of physical harming will not be the consideration, psychological harming should not be done in any way that must be kept in mind by the researchers. To do so if a situation demands anonymity of research participants, then it must be respected by researchers. For operational convenience names of the participants may be changed. Even if, a situation demands to maintain confidentiality in the form of not disclosing the identity of the research participants or their address, it must be ensured. Here needs the dedication of the researcher for being loyal to their participants, whatever situation arises researcher must keep the words that were given at the beginning to their participants. Even it is a liability of a researcher to share with his or her participants that how he or she is going to analyse the data. If it is not possible to explain all the technicalities, at least research findings or a summary of the research findings may be disclosed amongst the participants. Now it is almost compulsory to get a clearance certificate from the relevant institutional ethics committee. Sometimes novice researcher gets confused that how to get the clearance certificate from the ethical committee. There might be a chance of rejection in that case. It is better to structure a professional codes of ethics. If well-guided research ethics is available at the very initial stage of research, then it will not be a problem to maintain ethical consideration for the research participants.

Empirical Research Ethics

Empirical research is a kind of research where the researcher gets the first-hand experience from the field. During the interaction a researcher has to face several critical issues that come under the consideration of ethics. Some of the ethical issues mentioned by John and Lyn Lofland (1995:63). Generally, while interviewing a participant, the researcher tries to record the interview either by putting down the conversations or recording through a voice recorder. But it is a general practice to record the conversation without informing the interviewee. It is not to be done. The interviewee must be well aware that his or her voice is being recorded. It is also not an ethical practice to collect research information from a person with hatred. For the benefit of research, the researcher tries to suppress his or her emotions. Sometimes, the researcher indirectly collects information without approaching the target individual, it is not ethical also. A researcher has to commit always wholeheartedly to his or her respondents and must adhere to his or her words. For the benefit of the research, it is not good to be calculative for maintaining relationships with the research participants. Strategic moves may be the key to successful research but it is not an ethical move always. Taking a neutral stance is not always a good gesture, especially in a factionalized situation. It is better to take a side to clear the position of the researcher and to address the situation, especially when people are marginalizing or depriving. It is also not correct to bribe people to get research information if it is not admissible as an honorarium in the research. There is a common practice in empirical research to take the help of key informants or village headman for establishing a rapport with the informants or villagers. It is considered unethical to act in social science research because here researcher tries to play politics by influencing the decision-making process. In this regard, there is important writing by Guha, in which the ethics of the methodology of fieldwork were elaborately discussed in the study of Bengal Famine by Prof. T.C. Das (Guha 2011). This study shows how a sensitive social crisis can be studied keeping with all the social commitments.

Indigenous People and Research Ethics

Indigenous Peoples are the tribal peoples in independent countries whose distinctive identity, values, and history distinguishes them from other sections of the national community. Indigenous Peoples are the descendants of the original or pre-colonial inhabitants of a territory or geographical area and despite their legal status, retain some or all of their social, economic, cultural, and political institutions. the terms Indigenous, Aboriginal, Native, Indian, and First Nations interchangeably. These terms refer to the first peoples of Canada and, except First Nations. Indigenous communities are the sufferer of unequal power distribution in society. Some of them have experienced 'historical injustice' (Forest Rights Act 2006) as confessed by the Government, others are still on the verge of vulnerability. Indigenous people are considered as the repository of huge indigenous knowledge. Some of that knowledge is very much beneficial for non-indigenous societies. It is correct that this indigenous knowledge should be incorporated into everyday use. But it should be kept in mind that indigenous people are not well aware of their rights, especially their intellectual property rights. There are some guidelines for researching indigenous people (Indigenous Peoples Health Research Centre 2004). Anthropologists or any other non-anthropologists who work among the indigenous people must have certain ethical responsibilities to the studied communities. Since indigenous peoples are vulnerable, so some extra measures should be taken. Here, indigenous knowledge comes out to the outer world with the hand of researchers. It is the responsibility of the researcher to make sure the rights of the indigenous people over intellectual properties.

Intellectual Property Rights and Community Research

Every community has its cultural heritage. Some of them are tangible, whereas some of them are intangible. This intangible heritage is mainly folklores, literature, myths, riddles, rhymes, ethnomedicinal knowledge, and so on. Intellectual Property Rights (IPR) are a set of rights over intangible properties. Rights over community cultural heritage must adhere to the community members under IPR. So, the researcher who works on cultural heritage must keep in mind that it is the researcher's responsibility to properly acknowledge the cultural heritage. It comes under ethical consideration in social science research to make sure community rights over intellectual property. Since all communities are not legally equipped to claim their IPR, here it is a responsibility of a researcher. IPR does not only end with taking community consent or providing acknowledgement on IPR, it demands proper financial incentives also to the community members.

Apart from this, there is certain ethical consideration to be kept in mind by the researchers who work on communities. It starts from the early beginning with the research topic selection. It is the responsibility of a researcher to make sure that his/her topic would not harm any of the participants of the research. For example, evaluative research of a government scheme, might bring certain findings against the government or research on the behaviour of a sexual minority group might bring certain findings that are embarrassing for that group. In more sensitive research with individuals, research on trauma from violence, a refugee camp, or terminal experience, might put deep psychological distress over the participants. In all the cases, by judging the sensitivity researcher has to decide whether respondents or participants should be kept anonymous or not. As discussed earlier, if an individual research participant wants to remain anonymous, the researcher needs to respect the wishes of the participant.

At the time of publication of research findings, certain responsibilities arise with the researcher. That is to mention the names of all participants involved in the research with proper acknowledgement. Not only this, proper acknowledgement of all government and non-government organizations who played some role in providing research information. Even in the methodology section of the research report, ethical considerations must be elaborately explained. It may be mentioned with a certain declaration that how data will be preserved and accessible after research. Generally, it is expected that data will be well preserved and easily accessible for all and it has to be ensured through writing. Some academic ethical considerations have to be followed like mentioning all secondary references through proper referencing style. Above all not plagiarize from other sources for writing research documents without following referencing styles. After writing it has to be ensured that the circulation of the publication would be maximum. Last, but not least, that let the participants know what has been found from the research in which they took part.

Apart from textual documentation of research findings, there are some other modes of documentation of research, i.e., audio-visual documentation in the form of documentary filming. If it is based on community research certain ethical liabilities have to be followed by a filmmaker. Collection of consents from each participant for being part of the filming. Even, if a situation demands a mass gathering behind the subject, a set of consent may be collected through some mediators, like a local club or traditional village council. If the filming locality comes under the jurisdiction of a local organization or administration, clearance or permission may be collected from the concerned local authority. Sometimes, original music scores (collected from the field) are used in the documentary film, each score ownership must be uttered clearly in the acknowledgement section. If requires, financial incentives need to be paid to the owners of the original scores. Most of the time it is to be tried to get all the consent from the participants in a written format.

Realities

In India, in the case of social science research ethics boards are meagre in number. Hardly any transparency is found in the universities on how, where, and when to apply for ethical clearance. Even, supervisors are not all the time in a position to guide their scholars. So, the image of institutional ethical clearance is a little blurry in India. Whatever the existence of ethical boards is found in India, mainly they assess medical or biomedical research proposals. But in the case of qualitative research, ethics monitoring is not well equipped. In the case of intellectual property rights, it is not properly acknowledged by the owners. In the case of indigenous or rural or non-literate communities, the situation is worsening. Another area where the presence of ethical guideline needs to have a function efficiently, that is documentary film making on social issues. Most of the directors are not guided by any standard guidelines. It should be constructed through academic institutions in the form of small projects or dissertations. Though, academic institutions also suffer a lack of time or irregularity of institutional ethics board meetings.

Prospects

Indian culture is different from European culture therefore it is not expected that international ethical guidelines will be enough to secure the rights of the Indian participants. So, the locus of understanding ethical consideration should be community-specific. If it is not possible, at least region-specific ethical guidelines may be used in empirical social science research. In that case, Indian anthropologists can take initiative for structuring India specific qualitative research ethics. Anthropologists by profession, knowledgeable about community worldview, even they have the training of understanding community worldview. That background research may be useful for structuring the guideline on region-specific or community-specific ethical research guidelines. On the other hand, educating about research ethics to scholars is very much essential. So it must be compulsory in professional training. Not only that research ethics must be a part of the PhD course curriculum. With these future prospects of emprical research ethics, we could follow the words of Nelson Mandela (1996) that "we must work together to ensure the equitable distribution of wealth, opportunity, and power in our society".

References

Blocker, H. Gene. 1999. *World Philosophy: An East-West Comparative Introduction to Philosophy.* Prentice Hall: New Jersey. Pp.159.

DeVaries, R, & Subedi, J. (Eds.). 1998. *Bioethics and society: Constructing the ethical enterprise.* Upper Saddle River, NJ: Prentice Hall.

Forest Rights Act 2006. Accessed from <https://tribal.nic.in/FRA. aspx> on 7th January 2021.

Guha, A. 2011. Ethics of Fieldwork in the study of Bengal Famine: The Case of Tarak Chandra Das. *Journal of the Indian Anthropological Society,* 46: 135-143.

Gould, J.A. 1998. *Classical Philosophical Questions.* 9th ed. Prentice Hall: New Jersey.

Empirical Research Ethics 13

Heywood, A. 2017. *Politics.* Palgrave Macmillan: India.

Indigenous Peoples Health Research Centre. 2004. *The Ethics of Research Involving Indigenous Peoples.* Report of the Indigenous Peoples Health Research Centre to the Interagency Advisory Panel on Research Ethics

Lofland, J. and Lofland. L. H. 1995. *Analyzing Social Settings: A Guide to Qualitative Observation and Analysis.* 3rd ed. Belmont, CA: Wadsworth.

Mandela, N. 1996. 'State of the Nation Address'. Speech at Parliament, Cape Town, South Africa, February 9.

Mensch, P. 2014. *Herodotus Histories* (translated). Hackett Publishing Company: Cambridge.

Mitra, M. and Mitra, D. 2015. *Oxford English -English Bengali Dictionary.* Oxford University: New Delhi, India. Press. Pp.449.

Plato 2015. *Euthypho.* Prabhat Prakashan: India.

Rachels J. and Rachels, S. 2007. *The Right Things to Do.* (Ed.) Mc Graw Hill: New York. Pp.4.

Semple, J.W. 1871. *The Metaphysics of Ethics by Immanuel Kant* (translated). Lorimer and Gillies: Edinburgh.

Sullivan, T.J. 2000. *Introduction to Social Problem.* 5th ed. Allyn and Bacon: USA. Pp.137.

Tannsjo, T. 2002. *Understanding Ethics: An Introduction to Moral Theory.* Edinburgh University Press: Edinburgh.

World Health Organization 2009. *Research Ethics Committees: Basic Concepts for Capacity Building.* WHO Document Production Services, Geneva, Switzerland.

Zou, D. V. 2005. Raiding the dreaded past: Representations of headhunting and human sacrifice in north-east India. Indian Sociology (n.s.) 39, 1. SAGE Publications, New Delhi. Thousand Oaks/London.

CHAPTER – 2

Ethical Issues Relating to Fieldwork among Indigenous Communities

RAJAT KANTI DAS

Ethics are moral principles and values, which influence the way a researcher or a group of researchers conduct their research activities. Broadly it can be said that by following a system of moral principles researchers can judge how far their own actions in relation to others are right or wrong, good or bad, proper or improper. In anthropological field-based research particularly among indigenous communities, there is an added dimension to maintaining ethical codes. But first of all, the main issues concerning ethics should be identified. As stated by Rusli Ahmad and Hasbee Usop (2011), the following issues may be considered important at the initial stage. These are,

a. The rights of privacy of individual

b. Voluntary nature of participation by the individuals/ informants and their rights to withdraw from the process

c. Seeking consent from participants and their possible deception

d. Maintenance of the confidentiality of data provided by individuals or identifiable participants

e. Maintaining the anonymity of those providing data or information

f. Reactions of participants to the ways in which researcher seeks to collect data

g. Reactions of participants to the ways in which data are analysed and reported

h. Behaviours and objectivity of the researcher.

Based on the issues stated above, several checklists need to be considered by the researcher, which have direct implications to ethical issues in research. Some of these are given below:

a. Will the research process harm participant or from whom information is gathered?

b. Are the findings likely to cause harm to others not involved in the research?

c. Is the researcher violating accepted research practice in conducting the research and data analysis and drawing conclusions?

d. Is the researcher violating community or professional standards of conduct?

Clearly, the issues or points raised so far are general considerations applicable in the case of participatory research. In anthropological or anthropologically-oriented research ethical issues take diverse forms depending on the type, span and group(s) among whom research is to be carried out. Anthropologist's involvement in the field is much more intimate and close as a result of prolonged stay with the people, participating in their life activities and observing them from close quarters. This has advantages and disadvantages too. Anthropological research conducted among indigenous communities is now confronted with

16 *Research Ethics, Indigenous Communities and Fieldwork*

complexities that are as much a part of indigenous community itself as they are products of modern living marked by rapidly expanding inter-community network. Ethical issues concerning indigenous or tribal peoples are particularly concerned with the values relating to customary practices and usages. These are actually cultural values nurtured and grudgingly preserved by indigenous communities. One may wonder what exactly is the role of the Ethics Committee in research undertaken on an indigenous community? It is the Ethics Committee which now decides whether the conduct of each research proposal will protect the welfare and rights of participants including indigenous participants in the research and how far their privacy and confidentiality could be maintained. The researcher is to present material proof or evidence that provides a full and clear explanation of the proposed research, its justification, aims and potential benefits likely to be derived from it. The researcher is required to report adverse events or unexpected risks that may arise in course of the research. Side by side, it is also to be ascertained whether the burdens or risks associated with the research are worth taking; whether these are unfair or unjust. Not only that, steps to be taken to minimise risks need to be clearly stated. Measures to be taken to protect cultural sensitivities are to be worked out beforehand. When the research requires indigenous interpreters, the way one will deal with the issue of close kinship relations to potential participants in the research should be made known. If the research threatens social cohesion and collective life of indigenous communities, the researcher cannot avoid his or her own responsibility. Lastly, the researcher is to demonstrate the contribution of knowledge that is likely to follow from the research. The impression one gains from such an exercise is research is no

Ethical Issues Relating to Fieldwork among Indigenous Communities 17

longer the sole prerogative of the researcher; he or she is to be made accountable for all the steps undertaken or methods followed in the research and its likely consequences. Even after all these, the question remains whether the guidelines prepared by the Ethics Committee will be able to cover all types of research with the same degree of openness and clarity of purpose. This applies specifically to indigenous research in which anthropologists participate in a big way and their participation does not always follow a formal direction or set pattern. Research here is more an experience on the part of the researcher, which means it does not exactly remain confined within the fixed structure formally worked out by such a Committee. Much of the fervour of anthropological research on indigenous communities will be lost in the process of strictly adhering to a set of rules, propositions and procedural steps, which in a sense curtails the freedom of anthropologists engaged in such a form of research.

In the strictest sense of the term, an indigenous community has its own particularities, much of which has considerably been diluted or distorted in today's context. Even then, indigenous communities in the form of tribes or 'adivasis' (though all tribes are not indigenous) are endowed with specific characteristics of their own. But the strong 'social consciousness' which used to be the hallmark of such a community has been transformed into a type of political consciousness or ethnic consciousness, making the job of an anthropologist more difficult. This particularly applies to the legal or procedural part of the implementation of ethical codes. Ethics now interfere with the way anthropologists conceptualise 'social fields'. These fields could very well be identified as 'political arenas', which means they are characterised by some form of political authority having the ability to produce rules and to ensure their compliance. Where the government is in full control of the situation, it takes upon itself the responsibility to ensure their implementation to the concerned people. But the people as such may not be satisfied with the government action. In such a situation, what would be the course of action left to the researcher? There is a possibility that the researcher and his or her research findings may not be acceptable to the people if he or she is totally guided by the rules prescribed by the government. The ethical dilemmas faced by anthropologists are most visible when they are being increasingly questioned not only by those opposing indigenous groups to be given special status and attention but also by the representatives of the indigenous groups themselves who have been more conscious of their rights. With political autonomy and consolidation of ethnic identity gaining momentum among the indigenous people spearheaded by the emerging elites and political leaders, challenging questions are being asked which go right into 'the heart of anthropologists' own debate about professional ethics' (Veronia Strang 2003). If indigenous research is to follow its own methodological line of approach, ethical questions will also develop accordingly. The basic question is, as it has always been, whether anthropologists still retain the right to represent the 'other' in the form of indigenous groups or whether such representations should be controlled and directed by the people on whom they are conducting research. In today's perspective, it has become necessary to concentrate particularly on the political arena in which anthropological research is conducted. The new power dynamics now question the potential for objectivity in research as claimed by anthropologists while performing the roles of cultural relativists and as believers in an emic perspective. All of these may put the scientific credential of anthropology as a discipline to serious test. In order to address the ethical questions in the changed and changing situation, anthropologists are in need of making their research procedures objectively defined. Of course, this does not automatically place such a research in the objective category, but there may not be much scope for doubting its right intent and proper direction. What is more important is to remember that in qualitative research ethical questions are difficult to be objectively fixed so as to give them a universal character. Much depends on self-assertive individual behaviours, which often manifest violation of the basic moral and social values. On such occasions the job of an anthropologist as researcher becomes all the more difficult and the search for objectivity in research may appear to be a futile exercise. Ethics demand that the researcher should be able to prove his or her neutrality. Being guided by the demands of the policy makers, research institutions, funding agencies, how far it is possible for one to maintain neutrality remains a vexed question. To comply with the undue demands of the funding agencies to collect sensitive data, there is always the possibility for the researcher to incur displeasure of a group guided by its own moral standard. Discussions on ethical codes or ethics in general become meaningful 'at the moment of crisis, when they serve an essentially political purpose'. This is the contention of David Mills (1999), who thinks that the ethical questions are inextricably linked with politics. When anthropologists maintain that fact and value should be separated from one another, just as science and its application connote different meanings in different contexts, it obviously leads to a value-bifurcation in which science is seen as value-neutral and objective, which it is. When we accept anthropology as a scientifically-oriented discipline, doubts will always be there about how objectively we can judge the values. Anthropologists today may not be comfortable with indigenous values and indigenous people themselves may not be agreeable to their indifferent attitude. Still, evading any kind of association with science with its objective focus for the sake of accommodating different values pursued in a different situation may not be in the best interest of anthropology as a scientific discipline. As science is provided with more and more knowledge, it may be possible to draw conclusions from the more specific and secondary source, but these should have methodological significance in the sense that the overall approach is not particularly value-loaded. Moreover, one may also ask whether the values propagated by anthropology as a discipline reflect only those values shared by specific communities with a political agenda of their own or should it be so? Scientifically validated conclusions are based on a different set of values where rationality is the key.

Ethics in anthropological terms are particularly guided by the discipline's holistic approach. Pat Caplan (2005) suggests,' all aspects of the discipline: its epistemology, its fieldwork practices, and its institutional and wider social contexts' are not simply 'specialized interests'; all of these have wider implications and may not be seen in isolation. It implies that anthropological consideration of ethics is all pervasive and cannot be discussed in parts where social, economic, political or religious values operate at different levels, sometimes complementary and cooperative, sometimes antagonistic and opposing. In the context of fieldwork ethics and anthropology signify two types of relations: (i) the relations between anthropologists and subjects of their study; (ii) the responsibilities of anthropologists towards informants and all others associated with them. But there cannot be any particular yardstick or moral standard by which such relations could be judged and responsibilities could be fixed. Not unexpectedly, there will be differences between anthropologists and people they have studied. This equally applies to indigenous peoples for whom anthropology has a special place of importance. Today, the propriety of anthropologist as an 'outsider' making representations of indigenous culture has been questioned and contested by those people. Some of them have started questioning their findings, cast aspersions on their motive or even wanted direct material benefits from their relation with anthropologists, to whom these amount to violation of the moral standard or ethical codes defined in terms of moral values like truth, integrity, empathy and above all, human dignity. As has been made clear, the relation between anthropology and ethics tends to be dictated by power relations. Neither anthropologists nor the people involved are in a position to decide the course of action in their own terms. In this connection, Pel's (2000) advocacy for 'professional ethics' to follow a liberal approach so as to 'neutralise and depoliticise political relationships by constituting the self from the political interactions in which it necessarily has to operate' may not have many takers. Ethical principles in politically charged crisis situations tend to shift their position with regard to their contextuality and change in meaning. All in all, to follow a uniform pattern in applying ethical codes and principles in every situation may be a doubtful proposition. When we understand ethics as moral principles and values, the main point of consideration should be the way they influence a researcher or a group of researchers carrying out their research activities. It is generally believed that ethical problems faced by anthropologists in the field are partly their own making because of the fact that they carry with them their own moral values, which they find hard to dispense with. The problems faced by them sometimes follow a predictable line, which makes one think that as social beings humans everywhere react to violation of moral principles and associated values in almost similar manner. At this stage, the utility of a structural order binding individuals socially and mentally, best exemplified by the indigenous communities in their ideal form, cannot be undermined. Probably some form of objectivity could be achieved by pursuing a structural order at the experimental level, thereby making ethically-linked research more meaningful.

Much in line with diverse fields of anthropological interest, the ethical issues are also of diverse nature relating to specific fields of study like health, gender, ethnicity, food, demography and environment. Racism, discrimination and violation of the sovereign or distinctive existence of indigenous peoples may come within the purview of ethics, though issues also change their nature and character over time. Field situation today is much more fluid and as a result much more complex. Real indigeneity, however, tries to prevent such fluidity for its own interest. Under such circumstances, developing an anthropological perspective in terms of its own basic principles and priorities may run into difficulties. The merit of any anthropological study of an indigenous community cannot always be judged on the basis of the guidelines prepared by an Ethics Committee or an organization specially instituted for the purpose. Identifying or searching the roots of a code of ethics in 'the historical reality of relation between the studiers and the studied' (*Stephen Nugnet* 2003) may remain outside its scope. Ethnographic reality as demonstrated in the field may not be correctly reflected in the present scenario in which the anthropologist is required to play a mediating role not quite up to' the expectations of modern anthropological subjects'. Outwardly at least, there seems to be nothing unethical about it. But then modern anthropological subjects may include only a limited number of indigenes or their representation may vary from community to community. There are also reasons to believe that by aligning with the government the anthropologist comes under pressure from different quarters. When an anthropologist is in government service, he or she is required to follow the guidelines or restrictions imposed by the government on researcher's mode of behaviour to the concerned people. There are 'dos' and 'don'ts' to be maintained, which invariably affects the credibility of the researcher in the eyes of the people. Even otherwise, the freedom of anthropologist is curtailed hampering his or her free and at times uninhibited access to the people under study. Freedom here means freedom to choose one's method or mode of study by remaining true to the values nourished by the discipline. Such values teach one how to remain unbiased without being totally dispassionate, rational without being emotion free. For objective analysis we now depend more on records and institutions, which, though considered an invaluable basis for analysis, cannot be a better substitute for participant observation in anthropological research conducted among communities functioning more or less like a bounded system and guided by values of their creation. Long time back Harriet Martineau (1838a: Quoted from Bert N. Adams and R.A. Sidie 2001) gave a piece of advice to the observer to have "untrammelled and unreserved" sympathy towards the observed because an observer who could not find his or her "way to hearts and minds" of those under observation would be "liable to deception at every turn". Following Martineau, it may be further said that simple gestures and manners" cease to have meaning" if they are devoid of morals. This in a way sums up the justification for maintaining ethical standard in field-based research so important in anthropological understanding.

References

Adams, Bert N. and R.A. Sydie 2001. *Sociological Theory.* New Delhi: Vistaar Publications

Ahmad, Rusli and Hasbee Usop 2011. *Conducting Research in Social Sciences, Humanities, Economics and Management Studies.* Sarawak, Malaysia: RS Group Publishing House

Caplan, Pat (Ed.) 2003. *The ethics of Anthropology: Debates and dilemmas.* New York: Routledge

Mills, David 2003. 'Like a horse in blinkers': a political history of anthropology's research ethics. In: *The ethics of anthropology: debates and dilemmas.* edited by Pat Caplan. New York: Routledge

Nugent, Stephen 2003. "'Clubbed to death": anthropology, the Yanomami, Science and Ethics'. In: *The Ethics of Anthropology: Debates and Dilemmas.* Edited by Pat Caplan, London: Routledge

Strang, Veronica 2003. An appropriate question? the propriety of anthropological analysis in the Australian political arena. In *the ethics of anthropology: debates and dilemmas.* Edited by Pat Caplan. New York: Routledge.

CHAPTER – 3

Ethical Issues for doing Fieldwork among Indigenous People of India

K K GANGULY

It is very much essential to understand issues of indigenous/ tribal people of our country and more so the ethical issues involved in various indigenous centric research. A substantial number of indigenous people inhabit the Indian sub-continent.

The indigenous and ethnic people of the world have learnt to live in most hostile environmental condition in this universe. The most interesting feature associated with these indigenous and ethnic has been found that, they live in localities which are immensely rich in biodiversity. It is estimated that about 300 million indigenous people are living in world, out of which nearly half i.e. 150 million are living in Asia, about 30 million of which are living in Central and South America and a significant number of them are living in Australia, Europe, New Zealand, Africa, and erstwhile Soviet Union.

Indian Scenario

A substancial number of tribes have been placed under 'Schedule' as Scheduled Tribe by the Constitution of India.

The Himalayas stretching through Jammu and Kashmir, Himachal Pradesh, and Uttarakhand in the northwest, to Assam, Meghalaya, Tripura, Arunachal Pradesh, Mizoram, Manipur, and Nagaland in the northeast. In the north-eastern states of Arunachal Pradesh, Meghalaya, Mizoram, and Nagaland, more than 90% of the population is tribal. However, in the remaining northeast states of Assam, Manipur, Sikkim, and Tripura, tribal peoples form between 20 and 30% of the population. Other tribal peoples, including the Santhals, Oraon, Munda, and Ho live in Jharkhand and West Bengal. Central Indian states have the country's largest tribes, and, taken as a whole, roughly 75% of the total tribal population live there, although the tribal population their accounts for only around 10% of the region's total population.

Smaller numbers of tribal people are found in Odisha in eastern India; Karnataka, Tamil Nadu, and Kerala in southern India; in western India in Gujarat and Rajasthan, and in the union territories of Lakshadweep and the Andaman Islands and Nicobar Islands. About one percent of the populations of Kerala and Tamil Nadu are tribal, whereas about six percent in Andhra Pradesh and Karnataka are members of tribes.

The scheduled tribe population in Jharkhand constitutes 26.2% of the state (The Times of India, June 2013, Dailypioneer.com January 2017). Tribals in Jharkhand mainly follow Sarnaism, an animistic religion (Yadav A, Scroll.in, 2015). Chhattisgarh has also over 80 lakh scheduled tribe population (Bagchi, 2013, www.pib.nic.in, 2017, The Times of India, June 2014). Assam has over 60 lakh Adivasis primarily as tea workers (The Times of India, January 2015). Adivasis in

Indian tribes mainly follow Animism, Hinduism and Christianity (www.outlookindia.com, November 2017, Hindustan Times, December 2014).

Need of IRB for Indigenous People's Research

Tribal leaders, policymakers, researchers, and community members increasingly recognize the need for community participation in the regulation of research. Results from the 3-year intertribal IRB process confirm the importance of community involvement and Tribal sovereignty in the regulation process.

Ongoing efforts to educate policymakers and funding agencies about what constitutes research are needed to protect communities from risk. Honouring Tribal sovereignty requires that researchers be aware of the unique conditions and laws that govern Tribal nations. Community members should be involved in all aspects of the research process, and community-based participatory research approaches promote planning, data gathering, and dissemination of data; however, these approaches do not adequately address the need for community participation in regulation of research or in the review process.

Thus, the involvement of community members in a given research project, along with their relationship with the researcher, funding agency, and employer, must be considered. An intertribal board can reinforce the need for accountability; however, this requires a fundamental shift among all disciplines (health, ecological, educational, social, and political) in the ways in which research is developed and implemented in and with indigenous communities.

Regarding ethical issues of indigenous people's research, one need to be clear regarding certain factors i.e.

- Need to understand why the study is being carried out;
- Need to understand objectives, methods, and potential results of the research;
- Need to understand how the research will benefit their partnership and the field more broadly;
- Need to understand if and how the research could potentially harm their partnership;
- Need to understand that participation in the research is voluntary;
- Know that they can refuse to participate in the research and still be entitled to benefit from tribe and research-related activities;
- Opportunity of indigenous people for holistic involvement.
- Know that the research will respect the Code of Ethics and Integrity;
- Have the ability to ask the researchers questions about the research at any time;
- Contact the overall principal investigator if they have any concerns about an aspect of the research project.
- Ones they are part of the research they need to know certain factors regarding research.
- Research analyses, interpretations, and results must be presented to and discussed by all partners to ensure accuracy and avoid misunderstanding; mutual commitment to excellence and rigorous science;
- Integrity of indigenous knowledge and wisdom in all communities;
- Research must ensure confidentiality and anonymity of individuals, organizations, and communities unless

these parties choose to be named in the results (Accessed from: http://bit.ly/2FWgvdj).

Essentials Preamble of Indigenous Ethical Research

The probable miss during research among indigenous people. Different issues can arise, such as collecting informed consent from populations who are impoverished, illiterate, and hold high levels of mistrust of individuals from outside their community; the appropriateness of collecting individual consent among communities who maintain a collective identity; or the extent to which participation can be truly voluntary if individuals or communities lack the capacity to refuse participation.

In order to carry out ethically correct research among the indigenous people one need to take care of the following issues. Three potential strategies for strengthening ethical practices with STs are recommended here. First, to the greatest extent possible, research priorities should reflect the felt health needs of STs and their concerns, instead of being dominated by the interests of funders, policy-makers, research institutions, and researchers' own interests. This includes assessing the degree of correspondence between the main epidemiological and health problems identified among STs and the actual research being undertaken. Consulting with ST communities themselves should also be used to identify priority issues.

In order to reinforce ethically correct approach of research the indigenous people need to be partnered with the research team. The sense of stakeholder ship only grows with inclusive participation. Participatory approaches have been advocated as one way to increase the control of marginalized communities over their own research and policy priorities (Mohindra et al. 2011). Participatory approaches are rooted in the philosophy that those most affected by health and development issues should be active participants in the research process and how this research is translated into action, rejecting traditional scientific (positivist) approaches. To do justice without compromising the essence of research among indigenous people.

The researcher needs to remember certain aspects very vividly that the research among the tribal is not working with one individual. Tribe is collective noun and need to be handled accordingly. Should we thrust, on tribal communities, a value system premised on 'individualism' (most of the ethical parameters are individual centric) which potentially could disregard their 'communitarian' (most tribal actions are community based) value system. Is it not advisable to design methodologies that accommodate the socio-cultural practices of the communities being researched?

More efforts are needed to address the unique context of and considerations for Tribal regulation of the research process from an indigenous worldview. In the future, this may include state guidelines that honour indigenous knowledge. Education is needed for academics, students, institutions, funding agencies, and others about research on indigenous communities and publication of findings. This can be achieved through early discussions and ongoing communications with researchers about Tribal sovereignty and community protections. Researchers from all disciplines and backgrounds must be accountable to the community rather than only to their institution.

Reference

Bagchi, Suvojit. 2013. Chhattisgarh needs a tribal Chief Minister". The Hindu. https://www.thehindu.com/opinion/interview/

chhattisgarh-needs-a-tribal-chief minister/article5168478.ece retrieved on 26 September 2013. Ranchi News -

Dailypioneer.com 2017 Jharkhand's population rises, STs' numbers decline. https://www.dailypioneer.com/state-editions/ranchi/ jharkhands-population-risessts-numbers-decline.html retrieved 8 January 2017.

Feature 2017. pib.nic.in.https://pib.gov.in/feature/feyr2001/ fjun2001/f080620012.html retrieved 8 January 2017.

Hindustan Times 2002. In Jharkhand, tribes bear the cross of conversion politics. https://www.hindustantimes.com/india/ in-jharkhand-tribes-bear-the-cross-of conversion-politics/ storyc9nJ9EW2QGY9L7IM0RZhQO html accessed on 1 December 2014.

Mohindra, S. Katia, Narayana, Delampady, Haddad, Slim. 2011. Towards ethically-sound participatory research with marginalized populations: Experiences from India. Development in Practice 21(8):1168-1175. DOI: 10.1080/09614524.2011.590890.

Outlookindia.com 2002. Adivasi vs Vanvasi: The Hinduization of Tribals in India". https://www.outlookindia.com/website/story/ adivasi-vs-vanvasi-the hinduization-of-tribals-in-india/217974 published on 20 November 2002.

The Times of India 2013. Marginal fall in tribal population in Jharkhand. https://timesofindia.indiatimes.com/city/ ranchi/Marginal-fall-in-tribal-populationin-Jharkhand/ articleshow/20374392.cms retrieved on June 01, 2013.

The Times of India 2014. Population growth rate declines in Naxalite and tribal areas of Chhattisgarh.https://timesofindia.indiatimes. com/city/raipur/Population-growth rate-declines-in-Naxalite-and-tribal-areas-of Chhattisgarh / articleshow/36010452.cms retrieved on 03 June 2014.

The Times of India 2015. Why Assam's adivasis are soft targets | India News - Times of India". https://timesofindia. indiatimes.com/india/Why-Assams-adivasis-are-soft targets/ articleshow/45747349.cms retrieved on 04 January 2015.

10. University of Washington Research Ethics Training for Health in Indigenous Communities. Available at: http://bit.ly/2FWgvdj.

Yadav, Anumeha 2015. In Jharkhand's Singhbhum, religion census deepens divide among tribals". Scroll.in.https://scroll.in/article/754985/in-jharkhands-singhbhum religion-census-deepens-divide-among-tribals retrieved on September 2019.

CHAPTER – 4

Issues and Challenges in Conducting Ethnographic Research among Indigenous Communities in Bihar and Jharkhand

RAJEEV KAMAL KUMAR

Introduction

Anthropology is the spatio-temporal study of human beings. It includes the study of physical as well as social and cultural evolution of mankind. Since the work of Franz Boas and Bronislaw Malinowski in the late 19th and early 20th centuries, social and cultural anthropology has been distinguished from ethnology and from other social sciences by its emphasis on cross- cultural comparisons, long-term in-depth examination of context, and the importance it places on participant observation. Ethnography is one of its primary research designs as well as the text that is generated from anthropological fieldwork. The ethnographic method has now become even more relevant as with the advancement in technology, information and communication, modernization, and globalization, the human society has also been witnessing large scale changes in the society and culture, social structure, etc. This method is very useful in study of these changes. Realizing its importance, the anthropological methods are also being adopted by other social science disciplines for conducting the qualitative studies.

Several Anthropologists have advocated and also used ethnography as a research method in the study of human beings. According to Clifford Geertz (1973) anthropologists are mainly concerned with ethnography. Ethnography had its roots in cultural anthropology. All the early classical ethnographic studies were conducted to study the life and culture of some identifiable group in order to be able to construct a social reality and thereby understanding the social phenomenon in a much better way. It involves researching something closely, over time, in its natural setting, drawing on participation and observation, as well as other qualitative data collection techniques. The ethnographers generated understanding of culture through an *emic* perspective or what might be described as the insider's point of view. However, it is becoming increasingly important in the modern world. It has not only closed the gap between cultures, enabling people to better understand the true meaning and value of different customs and practices in once distant cultures but also has been extended to the researches across diverse disciplines (O'Reilly 2005, Bhomick 2014). Ethnographic approach is increasingly being used these days not only to study the society and culture of the indigenous people, but also in the field of public health, community medicine and even health systems (Tabatabaei 2016).

The main objective of present paper is to discuss the issues and challenges involved in conducting any ethnographic studies with indigenous population. It also offers some reflections and insights into the issues through two such studies conducted among indigenous communities of Jharkhand and Bihar in different time period by the researcher. The first study was conducted among Parhaiya of Chandwa block of Latehar district in Jharkhand state in a phased manner during 2002-04. The second study was conducted among two scheduled tribal communities i.e. Tharu and Oraon of Gaunaha block of West Champaran district in Bihar in the year 2015-16. The paper is organized into two sections. First section consists of a brief background of ethnographic studies and its relevance in studying human society and culture. The second part consists of a brief description of the studied communities and challenges faced in collecting ethnographic data with reference to the above two studies.

The significance of this study lies in outlining the importance of ethnographic method as one of the most important methods in understanding the society, culture and human behaviour. The ethnographic method has been useful in conducting in-depth studies among the indigenous communities in different cultural settings. It is mainly concerned with the approaches to the field and interaction processes that took place between researcher and studied community members to understand their society and culture. It also tries to highlight the issues and challenges faced by the researcher in conducting these studies.

Ethnographic Method

Social research is somewhat different from the general research. According to Young (1988), "social research is a systematic method of exploring, analyzing and conceptualizing social life in order to extend, correct or verify knowledge, whether that knowledge aid in the construction of a theory or in the practice of an art." This social research seeks to find explanations to unexplained social phenomena, to clarify the doubts, and correct the misconceived facts of social life. There are mainly two methods of study in social science- quantitative and qualitative. The quantitative method deals with the analysis and interpretations of numbers whereas qualitative method is concerned with text and context. Quantitative analysis also allows researchers to test specific hypotheses, in contrast to qualitative research, which is more of exploratory in nature. Qualitative method is grounded in a philosophical position, which is broadly "interpretive" that is concerned about how the social world is interpreted, understood, and experienced or produced.

The discipline of Anthropology, especially social/cultural Anthropology, is mainly based on the second type of research method. In this anthropological research method, the researcher gets a chance to trace historical events, their causes, long term consequences, and derive insightful explanations for all these events. It is all about understanding the context in which different events take place in the lives of a particular community under the study. The use of qualitative research methods in the discipline of Anthropology may be traced back to middle of 19th century when Franz Boas (1858-1942) used the field survey for his research work. He was a strong critique of Arm-Chaired Anthropologists and advocated for the need of field work to study the human beings and their society and culture. Later on, A.L. Kroeber, Bronislaw Malinowski, AR Radcliffe Brown, Margaret Mead, Ruth Benedict, etc., have taken this tradition of field work and qualitative study in Anthropology forward. It was Malinowski who has used the 'Participant Observation' technique for the first time while he was studying among Trobriand Islanders. Most of these Anthropologists largely dependent upon ethnographic method in conducting studies among tribal communities. Anthropology is a field based observational science, which studies the social life of the people from insider perspective or 'from within.' It is guided by its own distinct methodological orientation, which is an integral part of anthropological research. Anthropological approach is holistic which stipulates for the integrative, people-centred paradigm in which data and information are directly obtained through the method of fieldwork. Thus, fieldwork is central to anthropology or rather fieldwork sustains anthropology (Goode and Hatt 1981, Radcliffe-Brown 1983, Young 1988, Fetterman 1989, Doshi and Jain 2002).

The literal meaning of ethnography is to write about the people. It is the study of individual cultures and it is primarily descriptive and non-interpretive (Tylor 1991). It refers to the genre of writing that presents qualitative description of human social phenomena, based mainly on fieldwork and observation. Ethnographic approaches to data collection produce voluminous unstructured data from a range of sources, for example fieldwork note, diary entries, memos and where appropriate interview transcripts. Unlike popular belief, qualitative method can also produce a vast amount of data. In this, the researcher gets a chance to trace the historical events, their causes and long-term consequences and derive insightful explanations for all these events. Qualitative research is often referred as anthropological research simply because the kind of approach central to it is developed within anthropology, or it is also referred as field research or intensive field research or sometime as ethnographic research (Kumar, 2014).

Ethnography is not only a method but also a process and comprised of a set of methods using different tools and techniques at the same time for conducting the ethnographic study. These are observation, case study, in-depth interview, focused group discussion, field diary, etc. These tools and techniques are used separately or together at the same time to conduct ethnographic study. The researcher is involved in participating in certain activities among the studied population, also taking interviews or conducting FGD and making notes together at one point of time. Cultural anthropology and social anthropology were developed around ethnographic research and their canonical texts are mostly ethnographies e.g. 'Argonauts of the Western Pacific' (1922) by Bronislaw Malinowski; 'Coming of Age in Samoa' (1928) by Margaret Mead; 'The Nuer' (1940) by E. E. Evans-Pritchard; etc. Ethnographers are mainly participant observers.

Study Area and Communities

Before discussing challenges in conducting ethnographic studies among tribal communities, it is pertinent to mention basic ethnographic account of the studied communities and the area of study. First study was conducted among Parhaiyas in Latehar district of Jharkhand during 2002-04 and second study was conducted among two tribal communities namely Tharus and Oraons in West Champaran district of Bihar in 2015-16.

Parhaiya

An extensive fieldwork was carried out in Chandwa block of Latehar district in Jharkhand state during the year 2002-04 in phased manner. Chandwa block lies between 23.7° north latitude and 84.7° east longitude and its average altitude is 524 meters. There are 12 Gram Panchayats and 85 villages

Issues and Challenges in Conducting Ethnographic Research 39

in this block. For the present study, 11 Parhaiya Tolas (hamlets), i.e. Nagar, Damodar, and Kitta from Damodar Panchayat, Latdag, Sattgharwa, and Chatuag from Kamta Panchayat, Rud from Chandwa Panchayat, Rampur, Nakati Tola Serak from Serak Panchayat and Kitta (Sasang) and Sons (Dumariya Pani Tola) from Sasang Panchayat were covered. Most of the villages were located in the forest and hilly terrains and inaccessible.

The Parhaiya are indigenous people, living in the hilly and forest terrains of Jharkhand since time immemorial. They are mainly concentrated in Latehar and Palamau districts, but also scattered in the Hazaribagh district of Jharkhand and adjacent areas Bihar. Their real origin is not known, however, some British officials, during the Colonial Rule, (Hunter, 1867; Dalton, 1872; Forbes, 1872; Risley, 1891) have tried to study their society and culture for the purpose of administration. Later on, a few Indian Anthropologists (Prasad, 1961; Hari Mohan, 1975; Prasad, 1988; Dash Sharma, 1996; Kumar & Kapoor, 2009) have also studied this tribe.

The earliest official record about the Parhaiya is mentioned in the 'Annals of Indian Administration' by Hunter (1867), which describes Parhiayas as wildest people in Palamau along with the Birhor tribe. According to Forbes (1872), "the Parhaiya are a Hindi speaking aboriginal tribe, found in tolerable numbers in the more jungle parts of Pargana Palamau. In their habits and customs, they present a curious mixture of Hindu and the aboriginals, they are certainly not pure Mundas, but they may be "Kankus", who are branch of the Munda family". The Hindu section of the people believed that the Parhaiya are descendents of the Pandawas of the great Hindu epic Mahabharata and hence they are known as 'Pandawansi Parhaiya' (Prasad, 1988).

Parhaiya do not have the clan as such but their lineage system, which is of segmented nature, explains their social pattern. However, Risley (1891) mentioned some of mythical clan names – *Bagh* (tiger), *Giddh* (Vulture), *Faniga* (grasshopper), *Kauwa* (Crow), *Maina* (a bird), *Nag* (Cobra), etc. The lineage (*khut*) among Parhaiya is patrilineal. Segmentation within the lineage also occurs due to conflict of authority and lack of livelihood resources which leads to division and birth of a new village. This also happens when the lineage becomes bigger and older and thus forming a separate *tola* (hamlet) over time (Kumar and Kapoor, 2005).

Nuclear family is most prevalent. The authority of family rests in the oldest male member of the family but in some cases, the eldest son becomes the head (*karta*). Kinship holds important position in the absence of any clan system among the *Parhaiya*. They take kinship system into consideration at the time of settling a marriage. They take care of tribal endogamy and lineage exogamy while settling the marriage. Arranged marriages are most prevalent. Bride price ('*Sudama*') is also demanded, which consists of some cash, clothes for bride and household goods. Divorce is also found on the grounds of adultery, impotency, etc. *Parhaiya's* economy is largely dependent on food gathering and hunting (Prasad 1961; Dash Sharma, 1996). The forest is still one of the main sources of their livelihood as it provides bamboo for basketry, MFP, fuels, and other natural products. But now the economy of Parhaiya depends mainly upon agriculture, basketry, and wage labour. The Parhaiya combine the agriculture and year round collection of Minor Forest Produce (MFP) with their traditional occupation of basketry. Women also cooperate in earning the livelihood by assisting male members in the agricultural fields, collecting MFP, and fuel from the forests and doing basketry work besides looking after children and the household chores. Religion holds an important position in their lives. Their traditional festivals are Karma, Sarhul, Jitia, Sohrai, Holi, etc. (Dash Sharma, 1996; Kumar and Kapoor, 2004).

Tharu

The second study was conducted among two tribal communities namely *Tharu* and *Oraon* of Manguraha and Rupauliya villages respectively in Manguraha block of West Champaran district in Bihar. Manguraha is predominantly a Tharu village while Oraons are mainly concentrated in Rupauliya village. Manguraha village is located in the forest region of the Gaunaha forest, part of the Valmiki Nagar forest division. The village is situated on the foothills of Himalayas, on the eastern bank of Gandak River and across the river lies parts of Nepal. The nearest town is Narkatiyanganj. The district Headquarter, Bettiah is approximately 70 kms from the village. This village is largely cut off from rest of the world especially the urban areas of the district. There are three wards in the *Manguraha* village and all the three wards have the ward member from *Tharu* community. Of these, two are females and one is male ward member. In addition to *Tharus*, there are 27 other castes in the village.

Tharus are an ethnic group indigenous to *terrai* region (Southern foothills of Himalaya in Nepal and India). Among the two communities, *Tharus* are more dominant as they are the original settlers of the land. In due course of time, they have invited other tribal communities and occupational caste groups in the area such as barber, carpenters, iron smiths, etc., so that *Tharus* may avail their services in exchange. Although *Tharus* do not rely upon a single occupation but their traditional occupation has been shifting cultivation. They combine the agricultural activities with daily wage labour, domestication of animals, work as tailor, mason or labourers in factories, etc. The local area has very limited potential for job; hence they have to migrate outside. Now they have very limited access to the forest but it still plays important role in their lives. Some of them have also been engaged in the forest department as fourth grade employee (guard, driver, cook and animal trackers, etc.). Production is not specialized in nature and whatever produced is consumed by the family itself.

There are different sub-castes such as *Chaudhary, Kshatriya, Rana, Gurun,* etc. among them. They still adhere to the traditional system of family and marriage. The marriage takes place among the community members. *Tharus* belonging to the sub-caste *Chaudhary* and *Kshatriya* are considered superior. They prefer to take their partners from the same sub-castes but sometimes the marriages are also solemnized with other sub-castes. Young *Tharus* have limited liberty to take partners of their own choice as the most preferred form of marriage is arranged, which is mostly settled by the parents and elders in the family. The marriages are also settled in the neighbouring state of Uttar Pradesh and even in the adjoining parts of Nepal. Marriage is viewed as a contract and there is no prohibition on divorce and remarriage; kinship as an instrument of social bonds. They have traditional patriarchal society. Family structure used to be mostly joint system in tribal communities, but in recent past changes in family structure have also been observed. Kinship forms the basis of tribal social organization.

Oraon

The second studied village is Rupauliya, where another ST community –Oraon is primarily residing. This village is slightly nearer to the Gaunaha forest area. However, the distance between Rupauliya and Manguraha is hardly three kms, but Rupauliya is more inaccessible from the block and district headquarters, as there is no public transport facility which connects the village. They are living in this village for a number of generations. Their great grand parents have come to this village and settled down in one of the corners of the village. One of the respondents informed that the *Oraons* are living in this village since the year 1885 during the Zaminadari system. A few of them have the equivocal memory of the Zaminadari system and told that there were two landlords in the area –one was *Baba Morani* and another was *Jai Narayan Marwari*.

The social institutions of *Oraons* such as marriage, family, and kinship are still very intact and they have been following the same age-old systems of marriage and family till date. The marriage takes place among the same tribal members and arranged by the elders of the family and community. Conflicts in the *Oraons* society are not very uncommon. Oraons are mostly dependent upon the daily wage work and agricultural labour. Most of the families are either landless or have small pieces of land which is also not sufficient for enough production to meet the family needs round the year. They are also engaged in poultry and duck farming, domesticating pigs, goats, cows and oxen. The primary crop is paddy but also produce wheat, lentil, sugar cane, maize, and vegetables on small scale. They are also dependent upon the local forests from where they collect MFP, mainly woods for the fuel, raw materials for building houses. They also migrate outside in search of job as their village has limited livelihood resources and economic avenues. They do different types of unskilled work, mainly daily wage work in the brick kilns, stone cutting, *poldari* (labourer who are engaged in loading and unloading of materials), etc.

Conducting Ethnographic Studies among the indigenous communities...

As mentioned, both the above studies are primarily ethnographic in nature. Before starting any ethnographic study, meticulous planning is required, which includes developing a detailed research design, developing and finalizing the study tools, piloting the area and pre-testing the study tools, entry into the field and establishing rapport with the community, conducting in-depth interviews, formal and informal discussions, casual observations, etc. At each stage of the ethnographic study, the researcher may face several challenges and has to show extreme caution and patience in eliciting the information from the indigenous population.

The data for these two studies were collected by employing qualitative study tools and technique separately and in combination, because in the ethnographic study one cannot collect good and reliable data with the help of a single tool. However, the most effective technique in ethnographic study is observation, but interview schedule, FGD, case study, etc., were also used for collecting the data. According to Young (1988), "the aim of anthropological fieldwork is to grasp the native point of view, his relation to life and to realize his vision of world. And much can be learned about human behaviour by observing it, even at a distance." Observation may be influenced by preconceived theories. But all observation in ethnography is so influenced by preconceptions, and the preconceptions of the trained anthropologist are enormously less harmful than those of the average traveler or untrained though educated man on whom we had to rely in the past for information about uncivilized peoples (Radcliffe-Brown, 1983).

Although an Anthropologist is trained to become a keen observer, but the training alone does not ensure good field data through observation. It also depends much upon the instincts and intellects of the ethnographer in the field, i.e. how the ethnographer perceive and comprehend the field situation, and observes the nuances of social relations and exchange behaviour, inter-personal relationship, same routine lives of community members, tradition and culture etc., and how the researcher expresses the observed learning from the field. In these ethnographic studies, both observation and interview schedule were used extensively. Most of the interviews were conducted in the native language of *Parhaiya*, which is *Magahi* or *Magdhi* and Hindi was used among *Tharu* and *Oraon*. Most of these community members speak their local language as well as Hindi and hence communicating with them was not difficult, but communicating with the elderly people and women folk was more challenging, as they usually speak their own languages.

Research Design

While developing the research design for the above two studies, a few important factors, such as feasibility, organization of fieldwork, tools and techniques to be employed, time and its cost and finally its significance, were considered. "A study design includes at least the following component parts which are interdependent and not mutually exclusive: sources of information to be tapped, nature of study, objectives of study, socio-cultural context of study, geographical areas to be covered, periods of time to be encompassed, dimensions of the study, the basis for selecting the data techniques to be used in gathering data" (Young, 1988).

The first study was a little more challenging as *Parhiyas* belonged to PVTGs and resides in more isolated areas. Most of the areas, at the time of study, were also infested with *naxal* activities. Therefore, while designing the study, the villages were selected carefully. The second study has different kinds of challenges. First one was reaching the area. Most of the *Parhaiya* villages were isolated and there was no motorable road and public transport in the villages. Another challenge was locating the respondents and taking their time for interviews and discussions, as most of them were not available during the day time due to their temporary migration and working in the field. As these studies were ethnographic in nature, and hence more time was required to get the qualitative information from the study population. In case of the second study, the fieldwork and data collection were smoother as the forest guest house was used as base camp, which was in the Manguraha village itself.

Pilot Survey

The main aim of pilot survey is to finalize the study area (universe), pre-testing of the study tools and familiarity with the population to be studied and feasibility of the study. This is also essential for the acquaintance with area and people and establishing a good rapport with them, so that in subsequent visits, data could be collected easily without losing much time. The pilot survey for the first study was conducted for about one month; while for the second study two weeks were devoted. During the pilot visit, local officials at the district and block headquarters were also consulted. A few Anthropologists, who has worked among *Parhaiyas* were consulted to gain insight into the area and subject. In this regard various institutes pertaining to the subject namely Tribal Research Institute (TRI), Tribal Cooperative, and Ranchi University were consulted. Most of them discouraged the researcher and advised to change the area and, if possible, the tribe too. They held the view that the selected area (Latehar district of Jharkhand) is infested with naxal activities and the Parhaiya might have also turned to militancy. Although I was a little scared in the beginning but did not give up the topic as I was determined to take up the study and ventured into the area. At the block and village levels, a few key officials such as Block Development Officer (BDO), Block Welfare Officer (BWO), Circle Officer, Child Development Project Officer, Village Level Workers (VLWs), etc., were also consulted. Beside the government officials, panchayat members and officials of Non-Government Organizations of the area were also consulted. Different villages of *Parhaiyas* were also visited to make acquaintance with the community.

In the second ethnographic study among *Tharus* and *Oraons*, similar approach was adopted. The government and a few non-government officials were consulted before selecting the villages. Major information on the area, tribal population and their concentration were collected from them before moving to the villages for collecting data. Some key informants were also identified in this visit, which proved beneficial for the subsequent field visits, in gathering relevant data without losing much time and in establishing the rapport with the community. As mentioned the main aim of the pilot survey is to select the area and make acquaintance with the community. While choosing the area a few important factors were kept in mind including considerable tribal population, accessibility in terms of reach to the area and community, etc. Before moving to the field, study tools were prepared

48   *Research Ethics, Indigenous Communities and Fieldwork*

and further firmed up on the basis of the experience and information collected during the pilot survey.

Entry into the Community

Before making entry to the communities, all necessary preparations were made as gaining access to the community is most difficult part of ethnographic research. It not only allows the ethnographer to gather information but ideally it also provides acceptance as a member of the studied community for the time being. Initially there was some hesitation on the part of both- respondents and researcher in discussion and eliciting information especially the information related to the family and personal domain. But as time passes the community accepted the presence of researcher and started coming forward to provide information and discussion. It was realized that the informal and casual discussions with the community members were more helpful as these provided more insights into the studied communities' lives. I gained intimate knowledge and deep understanding of the context of social action and relations of the studied communities gradually as an insider.

During the first visit and subsequent interaction with Parhaiyas, it was found that they were shy in nature and peace loving. The Parhaiya soon became very friendly and forthcoming in providing information. Although the region is much prone to *naxalism*, I did not face much difficulty in conducting fieldwork. Just before undertaking the pilot study, the Chandwa block office was attacked and gheraoed by MCC men. The block officials were rescued only after arrival of additional security forces from the state capital. Since then a group of army personnel has been posted in the block campus.

Issues and Challenges in Conducting Ethnographic Research 49

Making arrangements for the stay in the field takes considerable amount of time. While making the stay arrangement at the field camp, certain factors need to be considered, such as, proximity and accessibility to the community, safety and security of base camp, etc. During the study of Parhaiyas, stay in the field was quite difficult as there was no hotel or rest house at block headquarters. For this the BDO of *Chandwa* block was requested to make arrangement. He arranged the community hall in block office premises. Although block office was safe from the miscreants as it is heavily guarded by the security forces, but there were no basic facilities such as toilet, proper drinking water, bed, food, etc., in the premises. The stay was quite difficult also due to the harsh winter and scorching summer and erratic electric supply. First few days were spent in collecting the relevant information and data from block office, veterinary hospital, primary health centre, district welfare office, etc. The detail information about Parhaiya villages was obtained from the block office.

The stay and food were not much a problem in study of *Tharus* and *Oraons* of West Champaran (Bihar) as there was a forest guest house at Gaunaha, which is very close to the studied communities and most of the basic amenities were available. We start the work very early and stay with the communities very late. It was almost living with the communities in their villages.

Sometimes the ethnographic field also provides opportunities to interact with complete strangers, who may not belong to the studied communities, but they have important information of the area and the communities. Spending time with them and casual discussion provide much in-depth knowledge on the subject. After a few days,

50 *Research Ethics, Indigenous Communities and Fieldwork*

the researcher had to share the room with a Junior Engineer of the block, who was just transferred from another block. I used to share my experiences of the field with him and in exchange he used to provide insights into implementation of different development programmes and schemes related to construction of houses, check-dams, etc. He used to explain the difficulty in implementing the schemes where MCC has profound impact and people are less aware of these programmes.

Another similar encounter was with a local contractor who gets petty contract works from the block office. He also has very good knowledge about the area and people and had very good rapport with the local *Parhaiyas*. He used to accompany me to the field and introduced to the respondents. Another key person in the field was the BWO, who was also staying in the block premises and in time of any immediate need I, used to approach him. He also accompanied me to some of the *Parhaiya* villages where he had to do inspection and prepare the list of beneficiaries including Parhaiyas for the ongoing schemes. We used to discuss about the programmes and schemes and its implementation.

Most of the time we choose a few key respondents, who are very helpful in the field in myriad ways, but sometimes we also come across them accidentally. These key informants are usually more perceptive, observant, informative, communicative, reflective and willing to give their time and share their knowledge about the area and community with the ethnographer. During the fieldwork, the identification of key informants depends largely upon the intellect of researcher. In these ethnographic studies, they proved of immense importance as a good amount of information were collected from them. Specific data and information like village history and its origin, social structure, social change, occupational mobility, etc., were collected from them. They were also helpful in introducing the researcher to the study communities and establishing good rapport with them.

Data Collection-tools and Procedures

The data collection in ethnographic study consumes a lot of time and requires huge patience of the ethnographer, as it is a gradual process, largely depending on the in-depth discussions with the respondents and community men and also participation in their day-to-day lives and casual observation. In the first study, both participant and non-participant methods were applied, but in second study non-participant observation was used due to paucity of time. The non-participant observation helped in gaining information on settlements pattern, house type, dress pattern, food habits, etc. As the time progressed and the rapport established, I moved to participant observation, which helped in gaining information related to social behaviour, social relations and customs, practices, etc., of the people. Notes were also taken in each phase of observation. While recording the observed phenomena, I specified those, which were unusual, and striking, which represented the specific details of information. For the first study, a total of 198 *Parhaiya* households covered and during the second study a total of 140 families (Tharu-74 and Oraon-66) were interviewed. These interviews were helpful in understanding the issues as these were largely structured but had a number of open-ended questions, which allow the respondents to put forth their opinions in details.

In addition to the observation and interviews a few case studies were also recorded in the field. Case Study is based on the personal interviews, observations of persons and families, documents and questionnaires. It is a holistic study of a well-defined or small social unit, which can be individuals (life history), institution, group, neighbourhood, or community. A few case studies were also recorded in the field. The aim of these case-studies was to discern information related to the characteristics of the groups and its mode of life to which the person under study conform or diverge, or clash and conflict; the characteristics which were unique to the individuals and distinguish them from others in the groups; types of available resources and types of problems. Genealogies of most of the respondents were also drawn in order to know the lineage structure, kinship structure and nature of institutions. This also helped in knowing the place of birth and migration after birth due to marriage or job.

Another very useful study tool used during these ethnographic studies was FGD. It is a focused and guided to some extent discussions among a group of people who are generally homogenous. The people participating in the discussion may likely to be benefited and affected by or related to the issues of the research. Besides ensuring homogeneity of group in terms of age, sex, educational level and other such attributes, the criteria of related issues of social structure, local customs and group dynamics were also considered. For these two ethnographic studies two groups of 8-10 persons of homogenous attributes were formed in each village and discussions were held. The groups were kept small so that interpersonal talks were avoided during the discussions and every member of the group was encouraged to put forward his/her opinions. The study tools, viz. FGD and interview were very helpful in cross-checking the observed learning.

Camera and recorder were also used, which helped in recollecting of every detail of the field. These aids proved helpful in capturing the characteristically significant behavioural events in their situational contexts. However, these audio-visual aids were used very sensibly in a limited manner, so that the respondents did not become conscious.

Inter-Cultural Communication

Establishing good rapport with the studied community is must for conducting any authentic ethnographic study. Communication plays important role in establishing rapport. Sometimes, there is a wide cultural gap between the studied community and the researcher. Here, the inter-cultural communication (communication between two cultural groups) plays important role in moving ahead. Interaction with the *Parhaiyas* during the fieldwork was quite comfortable, as the researcher comes from the different culture group but belong to same linguistic group. I used to converse in the local dialect, which is similar to Magahi/Magadhi and due to this my mind was in communion with them. This inter-cultural communication helped a lot in one or other ways like in establishing rapport and gaining the faith of Parhaiya. Most importantly, the first hand, reliable data were gathered without the help of any interpreter. However, most men were well conversed in Hindi, but the old people and women used to converse in Magahi only. In order to get closer and friendly to the local people the local dialect was opted and the interviews were also conducted in the Magahi, which helps in easy conversation and smooth flow of information.

Issues and Challenges in Conducting Ethnographic Study

Approaching the community and communicating the purpose of research: The first and foremost problem in ethnographic study is communicating with the indigenous people. This is even more difficult when the studied community belongs to PVTGs, as they are mostly illiterates, isolated from the mainstream society, shy in nature and avoiding any outside contact, hesitates in contacting and communicating others and also having less exposure to the outside world. Maintaining veracity of ethnographic study could be difficult in literal sense, as the researcher often failed to communicate the exact purpose of the research to the respondents belonging to the indigenous population. In the above field situations, I tried to adhere to the morale of eliciting the relevant information adopting the standard procedures, without any bias to the study population in any manner.

Establishing rapport and gaining trust of the study population: The data for any ethnographic study in Indian setting could be collected only after establishing proper rapport with the community. In this scene the researcher may or may not able to convince the exact purpose of the study, but gaining the trust is more important. The usual prescription for conducting any ethnographic study, or even any anthropological study, is communicating the exact purpose of the research with the study community. The researcher has to address the ethical issues which may arise out of the proposed study. It may also arise due to different cultural backgrounds and values and humanistic aspects (Tabatabaei, 2016). However ethical issues in this kind of research are also a debatable issue, as it is difficult to define its exact nature (Daniel-McKeigue, 2007). Broadly ethics can be considered as a body of moral principles or standards of human nature that conduct the behaviour of individual in correct path. However, this kind of dilemma was faced by the researcher in conducting the above two studies, but the guiding principle for these studies was the standard practices of data collection in Indian setting. The respondents were told about the purpose and whatever information was required was taken with full consent. The respondents also had the liberty to deny the interview, sharing information and opt out during the interview. They were not disturbed in their regular works.

Cultural differences between the researchers and study populations, who may belong to indigenous community: Sometimes the culture setting is also a barrier for not only the study population but the researcher as well. Even for the well-trained and well-prepared ethnographers, the field situation often offers a piqued condition, as every field situation is unique and what comes in the field is unknown to the researcher. In the field situation, both the researchers as well as study population belong to different cultural backgrounds, and this varied cultural setting offers challenges for both. It is not only on the part of the study population that they show some kind of apprehension and inhibition in divulging the information, but the researcher also had some cultural inhibition in interacting freely with such group of respondents.

Expectation of the community members from the researcher: In every anthropological fieldwork, the researcher has some definite purpose and expectations from the field situations. Sometimes this expectation is from both the sides, i.e., from researchers as well as respondents. The researcher expects quality data which is suitable to the purpose and objectives of the study. Similarly, the respondents have different expectations from the researchers. While conducting the first study on development programmes on Parhaiyas of Latehar in Jharkhand state, some of the respondents come

56 *Research Ethics, Indigenous Communities and Fieldwork*

to the researcher with some expectations to get some sort of help in availing the development schemes from the government. Since most of the Parhaiyas are illiterate and hesitant to contact the block development officials, they used to come to the researcher. This happens despite the clear communication of the purpose of the research. In other studies as well among the indigenous communities of Bihar, it was found that the respondents come to the researcher with similar expectations. Lonely and aged respondents also come to the researcher to narrate their woes and miseries and with expectation of a little help in one form or other from the researcher. Some of the questions in the interview schedule, such as questions related to the economic condition, livelihood resources, monthly income, status of livestock in the family, etc., invite the attention of the respondents. For this, the other community members and villagers who are not included in the sample would also come to the researcher enquiring about the purpose of the visit of the researcher and some of them even request to offer their time for the interview. They often insist on filling the form (conducting interviews) for their families as well. This also happens during casual discussions with the respondents.

Pragmatic participant observation: Ethnographic methods are diverse and a range of approaches can be adopted, they are based on observation, often complemented with interviews, and detailed analysis often at a micro level. Participant observation requires immersion in the setting under investigation, observing the language, behaviours and values of the participants. In the above mentioned two studies, the researcher has chosen to adopt 'observer-as-participant'. Stay during the entire fieldwork for the first study was inside the block office. Since most of the villages are isolated and situated at a considerable distance and *Naxal* affected, it would be very risky to stay in the village itself. However, the researcher has given ample time in the field, but full immersion and going native was very hard to achieve. For this, the selective participation was adopted for the data collection, which was also validated with individual interviews and discussions with the respondents.

To conclude, it could be said that the ethnographic study presents challenges and the stricter norms of ethical practices may sometimes ignored by the Indian ethnographers. However, there should be a middle path for conducting this type of study among the Indian aborigines, where the standard ethical practices should be considered as per the local cultural setting.

References

Bhowmick, S. 2014. Ethnography: A Tool of Research. *Man and Life*. 40(1-2): 119-142.

Dalton, E.T. 1872. Descriptive Ethnology of Bengal. Calacutta: Govt. of Bengal. (Reprinted 1960).

Dash Sharma, P. 1996. The Parhaiyas of Palamau: An Ethnographic Study. Ranchi: Bihar Tribal Welfare Research Institute.

Doshi, S.L and P.C. Jain 2002. Social Anthropology. New Delhi: Rawat Publications.

Fetterman, David M. 1989. Ethnography Step by Step. Applied Social Research Series, Vol-17. New Delhi: Saga Publications.

Forbes, L.R. 1872. Report of the Ryotwaree Settlement of Government Farms in Palamau. Calcutta: Bengal Press Secretariat (Reprinted 1970).

Geertz, C. 1973 The Interpretation of Cultures. New York: Basic Books, Inc. Publishers.

Goode, William J. and Paul K. Hatt 1981. Methods in Social Research. New Delhi: McGraw-Hill Kogakush Ltd.

Hari Mohan 1975. *The Parhaiya: A Study in Culture Change*. Ranchi: Bihar Tribal Welfare Research Institute.

Hunter, G. 1867. The Annals of Indian Administration. Vol. VI, Part II Calcutta.

Kumar, S. 2014. Ethnographic Research: Holistic Understanding of Human Behaviour Through Text and Context. Jharkhand Journal of Development and Management Studies, XISS, Ranchi. 12(1): 5709-5730.

Kumar, Rajeev. K. and A.K. Kapoor 2009. Management of Primitive Tribe: Role of Development Dynamics. New Delhi: Academic Excellence.

Kumar, Rajeev. K. and A.K. Kapoor 2005. Social Organizations in Parhaiya: A Primitive Tribe of Jharkhand. Man and Life. 31(1-2): 53-60.

Kumar, Rajeev K, V.C. Channa and A.K. Kapoor 2006. Role of Government Programmes in Parhaiya: A Primitive Tribe o Jharkhand. In, Anthropology of Primitive Tribes of India: The Changing Facets, P. Dash Sharma (ed). Delhi: Serial Publication.

O'Reilly, Karen 2005. Introduction to Ethnographic Methods. NY, Routledge.

Prasad, N. 1961. Land and People of Tribal Bihar. Ranchi: Bihar Tribal Welfare Research Institute.

Prasad, R. 1988. Tribes A Study in Cultural Ecology and Tribal Dynamics. Delhi: Amar Prakashan.

Radcliff Brown, A.R. 1983 The Methods of Ethnology and Social Anthropology. In, Method in Social Anthropology, M. N. Srinivas (ed). PP.3-38. Delhi: Hindustan Publishing corporation.

Risley, H.H. 1891. The Tribes and Castes of Bengal. Calcutta: Govt. of Bengal.

Tabatabei, S.Z. 2016. Ethical Issues during Ethnographic Research in Residential Homes: A Personal Experience JOHE, Spring 5(2): 121-128.

Tylor, E.B. 1991. Dictionary of Anthropology. Delhi: Goyal Publishers & Distributors.

Vidyarthi, L.P. 1982. Problems and Prospects of Tribal Development in India. In, Tribal Development in India Problems and Prospects, B. Chaudhuri (ed). PP. 375-340. Inter-India Publications, New Delhi.

Vidyarthi, L.P. and B.K. Rai 1985. The Tribal Culture of India. Concept Publishing Co. Delhi.

Young, P.V. 1988 Scientific Social Surveys and Research. New Delhi: Prentice Hall of India Pvt. Ltd.

CHAPTER – 5

Ethical Issues with Indigenous and Non-Indigenous Populations: Some Considerations

GAUTAM KUMAR KSHATRIYA

Ethical issues with Human Populations

The attribute of being ethical is an outcome of bio-cultural evolution. It is furthered by cultural norms and social teaching to develop the attribute of fellow feeling among the individuals for a peaceful coexistence and to protect the rights of individuals, particularly the vulnerable and weaker sections of the society. It is the worldview of the whole humanity through civilization, which has been inculcated in the process of time as per belief system.

In the evolutionary process of human civilization, the sociality led to the development of human societies against every odd during primitive time. Group living becoming inseparable character in human struggle for existence led to the evolution of band society. To keep the band together, certain normative principles were devised which later on were elaborated to develop morals and ethics.

Society not only ensured provision of food security to its members but also took care of the children, women and physically infirm Kinship gave more strength to the society by introducing obligatory relationship. Altruistic behavior was encouraged. Difference between 'right' and 'wrong', 'sin' and 'virtue', 'moral' and 'immoral' acts were defined by collective wisdom of the society, comprehensive and acceptable to all the members. As Henry Rink observed in his studies among the Eskimos that any act or behavior by any member of the band or society detrimental to the interest of other person, by failure to observe them, brings upon the offender the contempt of the whole tribes, and he runs the risk of becoming an outcaste and being banished from his clan. Otherwise, the offender might bring up the displeasure of the wronged animals, or of the spirits of the ancestors who protect the tribe (Rink,1887). Truthfulness is an essential virtue for the member leading group life under natural conditions. Morality was made infused into a person and made a part of 'conscience' or inner self. Breach of morality is a sin which goes against natural system. Any willful or inadvertent violation of social rules constitutes offence.

As human mind developed through time, the societal structure and its management system became more complex. Experiences were piled up per generation, old rules were amended and new rules introduced. In all cases, the ultimate objective was to benefit most members and uphold personal dignity and rights of the members of the society.

In different areas of the earth, different environment prevailed, encouraging the human societies to frame rules appropriate to thrive in those conditions. Since the rise of civilized societies, ethical principles were followed and those who flunked the accepted norms were 'barbarians'. Ethics dictated hunting practices and warfare. Ethics, protected the natural rights of all, whether a friend or foeman or animal.

This sociality is the primary base of mutual respect, the basis of morality or in other sense, the human rights. With the appearance of the religion, even in its crudest form, human ethics was enriched by a new element, which gave to the ethics certain stability. With further development of social life, the conception of rights and justice in mutual decisions had to become more and more prominent .Justice is necessary in mutual relations and it had to be made by Man for the sake of the preservation of social life itself promoting the rights of the participants in the society. And truly, in any society. Such collisions would inevitably lead to endless feuds and to disintegration of the society, if it were not that human beings develop a conception of the equality of right of all the members of the society (Acharya et al. 2015). In this context the rights of Indigenous Populations (IPs) become extremely important. Before we consider ethical issues in the context of IPs, it is necessary to explain as to who could be classified as Indigenous People

United Nations criteria has laid down following criteria for distinguishing Indigenous Peoples;

- Residence within or attachment to geographically distinct traditional habitats, ancestral territories, and natural resources in these habitats and social identities

- Maintenance of cultural and social identities, and social, economic, cultural and political institutions separate from main stream or dominant societies and cultures

- Descent from population groups present in a given area, most frequently before modern states or territories were created and current borders defined (ancient groups)

- Self-identification as being part of distinct indigenous cultural group, and display of desire to preserve that cultural identity

UNDP notes that self-identification is most fundamental criterion for determining indigenous or tribal groups in combination with other variables such as language spoken and geographical location or concentration. Besides kinship system can also be considered as most important aspect of tribal identification. (www.who.int/ethics/indigenous_peoples/en/index10...)

When we talk about ethical issues it is seen that ethical review is weak or non-existent in some developing countries and marginalized populations are not familiar with research management procedures or the ethical requirements of the research process. In India, ICMR (2017) has brought out a comprehensive document on " National Ethical Guidelines for Bio-medical and Health Research Involving Human Participants" of around 170 pages. Unfortunately, we do not follow the guidelines in letter and spirit, and many of us flaunt these norms and do not follow verbatim.

It is imperative that tribal groups should be imparted the provision of National and International guidelines by holding seminars at National, State, or local levels. We are lagging behind in this context

In case of health related issues research should be undertaken only if it has potential benefits for the local population. More often, such information is restricted to publications and organizing seminars etc. Care should be taken that they are not exploited economically by the outside organization. This is a particular concern in genetic research. A meaningful informed consent is one way of protecting against such exploitation. Special care has to be taken that consent is truly informed and that individuals and groups thoroughly understand what is being proposed and why (www.who.int/ethics/indigenous_peoples/en/index10...). In India we are not up to the mark in addressing both scientific and the ethical dimension of the research in practice although we have ICMR guidelines and to some extent DBT advisories too.

It may not be out of place to state that IPs have been involved in many genetic ancestry and health related projects. Their participation has been sought out on the basis that their genetic material is highly informative for the study of population history and disease, but also because they may benefit, particularly from the genetic studies of rare heritable diseases that affect their communities. However, IPs involvement has often resulted in lot of acrimony

IPs have expressed concern that that they do not benefit from genetic research, that genetics diverts attention and resources from non-genetic causes of health disparities including racism and that genetic research could reinforce racism by implying that IPs have genetic susceptibilities to disease and are thus inherently unhealthy. (Kowal, 2015)

In fact, many population genetic studies on genetic isolate have ended up with the same inferences. Moreover, many times there is lack of involvement of IPs in the planning of projects and many times planners are insensitive to cultural beliefs in the practice of research. Experiences of dispossession, marginalization, and oppression have led many IP to distrust science and the dominant society. Classification and stratification of IPs by science has increased the suspicion of genetics. In Australia, the assimilation era (1930s-60s), the state sought to breed 'out the color' and make aboriginal and Torres Strait Islander People 'White' through the

Ethical Issues with Indigenous and Non-Indigenous Populations 65

removal of children of mixed heritage from their families (Kowal, 2015).

More recently, genetic research on IPs has spurred a number of controversies. It is evident from following two case studies (Kowal, 2015).

Havasupai

They are native Americans who live in the base of Grand Canyon in Arizona. In early 1990s a genetic research was initiated into diabetics, as there was concern about the rate of amputations among the community members. Researchers obtained a broad written informed consent for 'medical/behavioral research' when blood samples were collected.

Samples were used for a number of other studies without specific consent, including one into ancient population migration in to the America from Asia.

The Havasupai discovered that their samples have been used in this way when a member of the tribal community attended a seminar organized by Arizona State Universty TSU) in 2003.Tribal members felt that this research contradicted their cosmological beliefs and threatened their sovereignty. The samples were also used for schizophrenia that had the potential to stigmatize their identity. They initiated a legal action against ASU and finally 151 remaining samples were returned to Havasupai.

Yanomami

Anthropologist Napoleon Chagnon and geneticist James Neel collected blood samples from the Yanomami in Brazil and Venezuela in the 1960s and 1970s. The samples have been held since that time at various laboratories in the USA. Both of them have been accused of unethical research practices in dealing with the Yanomami.

One of the reporters accused that the vaccination campaign developed by the team of Chagnon and Neel actually did more harm to worsen the measles epidemic that eventually devastated the population than it did to help prevent. It was claimed that they actually started epidemic by using vaccine too virulent for that particular population. Neel was accused of purposely starting this epidemic so he could observe the effects of an epidemic on a population and to study some of his ideas about eugenics. Accusations have not been proven.

However, Yanomami began a campaign for the return of their samples on cultural ground. When a Yanomami dies, their body is cremated and no physical remains orthe possessions of dead are kept. In this way, Yanomami ensure that deceased departs the world and separate the world of living from the world of the dead. A blood sample kept in freezer may prevent this process of occurring. The Yanomami requested for the return of samples so that samples may be ritually destroyed by Shamans and elders. Unfortunately, so far the samples have not been returned due to many bureaucratic hurdles.

Many indigenous belief are associated with blood samples across the tribal societies of the world which are in direct contrast to modern understanding.

This raises the question of the role of anthropologist in a conflict situation between IP and the governments of the countries in which they reside. Should the anthropologist be an objective observer, an advocate or neither of these?

Indigenous cultural beliefs about human origins are another source of contestation between scholars and IP. Cosmological beliefs of many indigenous cultures indicate that group was born where it is now ; and did not migrate to

Ethical Issues with Indigenous and Non-Indigenous Populations 67

their traditional lands from elsewhere. Scientists believe that Afrca is the cradle of human existence and Homo sapiens migrated to other parts of the world some 100,000 years ago (Kowal, 2015).

This conflict is especially intense when it comes to North America; where Native Americans are particularly not happy about the scientific explanations of their origin from East Asians who migrated to north America some 15000 years ago via Bering Strait. (Foster and Sharp, 2000).

Many argue that scientific accounts of the population history threaten indigenous peoples land claims and their sovereignty rights (Harmon, 2010). These observations are certainly part of ethical issues. Further, ethically it is the duty of anthropologist of preventing any potentially harmful information having negative impact on our informants. During the World Wars, the CIA employed anthropologist to learn about enemies to figure out how to best defeat them. This is unethical. But, anthropologist is still employed e.g.in middle east where there is conflict. But it is little tricky. And the objective is rephrased i.e. how to successfully interact with these groups to avoid conflict. (core.ecu.edu/anth/leibowitzj/2methods.html)

Then, many of the issues specific to IPs can be understood through the concept of group harm

A study that found lower than expected Native American ancestry among the participants is potential to create conflict among different segments of the tribe who questioned whether such participants had required blood quantum for tribal membership. A research finding that a group is susceptible to a particular disease has the potential to increase discrimination against the IPs. In this context a a research on the genes related to enzyme monoamine oxidase-A (MAO-A) in Maori tribe of New Zealand is very important. It is found that a variant of MAO-A gene has been associated with risk taking and aggression and is consequently known as "warrior gene". The study was widely reported as a proof that Maori were genetically predetermined to be violent. A Maori academic argued that the result was scientifically unsound, contributes to racial stereotyping and may lead to genetic and racial discrimination by insurance companies (Hook, 2009).

There are many genetic disorders or cancers of various type which are associated with different genes or variants so is it ethical in bio medical sciences to terminate pregnancy on mere suspicion that the baby in future may be susceptible to develop the disorder in case of mere association?

Understanding the ethical issues related to indigenous genetic research is important to uphold the rights of indigenous people. It was noticed in Peru that biological samples were provided to the laboratories across the country without the consent or even knowledge of the research subjects, which was a clear violation of human rights. IPs have often been vulnerable to research exploitation (Minaya and Roque, 2015)

Many ethical issues also arise with private corporations. Brent Berlin an anthropologist has been bitterly criticized because his association with pharmaceutical companies. He has been accused of bio-piracy.uncommon for an anthropologist. His focus is on medicinal plants and he works in Chipas, Mexico.

Part of his funding comes from pharmaceutical companies to uncover plants that may be used for new medicines. The controversy is that IP believe that their intellectual property rights are being violated. Basically controversy is due to the fact that the group with whom Berlin is working is getting benefit while other groups who have the same knowledge are not getting the benefits from the knowledge being used by these large corporations. Berlin is accused of exploiting the native populations of the area, because he is bringing large pharmaceutical company (core.ecu.edu/anth/leibowitzj/2methods.html). It is again an ethical issue.

Illegal Drug Trial and Human rights Violation, Indian Situation: (Acharya eta. 2015)

Major pharmaceutical complaints from around the world are conducting trails of their newly released drug on patients in underdeveloped and developing countries. Most of the Asian and African countries are the destination of such trials fore these multinationals as the poor and less informed patients of such countries are being posed as guinea pigs. The loosely structured drug regulatory system allows such practices. Certain incentive hungry physicians are prescribing such drug applications practices and simultaneously are reporting the results to the respective pharmaceuticals. Particularly the very poor monitoring of adverse drug reactions is a matter of serious concerns. It is highly unethical on the part of drug producers and immoral for doctors to use ignorant poor patients as experimental subjects. The issues of suffering s, deformities and death of these powerless people are not being addressed at all or are addressed partially. The guidelines of biomedical ethics have remained as simple formalities.

There are going on many such medical trials and experiments where the consent of the subject or his/her relatives was not taken. Few of the many such violation of human rights during medical trials which were much publicized and highly criticized are worth mentioning here.

The case of illegal clinical trial of anti-cervical cancer in Andhra Pradesh and Gujarat

A serious issue of illegal clinical trial of an anti-cervical cancer vaccine came to the news in the year 2011 and was widely discussed and criticized in public forum. The Documents show the large scale clinical trial was conducted on 24,000,10-14 years girls, mostly belonging from tribal community in Andhra Pradesh and Gujarat by MSD pharmaceuticals Pvt. Ltd. and GlaxoSmithKline Ltd. with the help of an Indian NGO named PATH. Four of the 14,091 in Andhra Pradesh , two of the 10,686 in Gujarat died (Mudur , 2010).While company in the home page of its website has mentioned that the duration of protection of Gardasil, the tried vaccine has not been established. This phase IV trial based on a study carried out on just 110 children by foreign pharmaceuticals companies not registered in India. Indian Council of Medical Research "provided technical support for the development of protocols and advised on ethical issues". While ICMR first denied the deaths due to illegal trials, violation of Indian biomedical ethics guidelines was observed by the expert committee later and was confirmed by Union Health Minister

The case of drugs in Regional Cancer centre in Thiruvananthapuram, Kerala

The RCC's collaborative venture with the U.S. based Johns Hopkins University (JHU) to test the effectiveness of certain chemicals as anti cancer drugs seems to have the ubiquitous flaws, right from the beginning : it failed to address the primary

Ethical Issues with Indigenous and Non-Indigenous Populations 71

duty of preventing the abuse of research subjects with or without knowledge (Acharya *et. al.* 2015). It was claimed that an investigational drug was injected into cancer patients at the Regional Cancer centre (RCC) in Thiruvananthapuram, the state capital without, clearance from the Drug Controller General of India and without approval from the institutional ethical committee (Jayaraman, 2001).

Illegal drugs trial on industrial gas leak disaster

Bhopal a central Indian city witnessed one of the worst industrial disasters of the world in 1984 from a deadly gas leak killing about 20000 and leaving many more incapacitated. About 30 years suffering from the happening of this tragedy the illegal drugs trial came to the survivors as a new disaster at personal as well as emotional level that these people have been again put to an illegal drugs trial. It was revealed that a number of drugs under trial were administrated on the patients without the informed consent or under reduced autonomy in Bhopal Memorial hospital and Research center (BMHRC) and out of 279 people under the trial, 215 were gas survivors while the further report says at least 10 gas victims died while they were on these drugs. As per the inspection report by Central Drugs Standard Control Organization (CDSCO), out of 26 clinical trials conducted in this hospital, 23 trials had irregularities by violating good medical practice norms.

India is turning into a hot destination for drug trails where patients are being administered the trial drugs or vaccines many a times without their consent.

India has several advantages a host for such trials. Its biggest asset is probably the size of its population it is more than 1 billion. In addition Indians are suffering from the same illness as Americans and Europeans-diseases for which companies are desperate to find cures.for instance at lease 70 millian Indians suffer from heart disease and 35 million have diabities. It also has the edge over most developing countries because of its sophisticated hospitals and because many of its medical personnel speak English (Aacharya *et al.* 2015). In 2003, private clinics across India used a generic version of the anticancer drug letrozole to treat more than 435 women with fertility problems. This trial did not have clearance from the health ministry, and the women involved did not know that the drug was not approved for this use. The manufacturer, Mumbai-based Sun Pharmaceuticals, denies ordering this trial (Padma, 2005).

Not only this around 3000 deaths was recorded during government approved clinical trials of new drugs, 89 were directly linked to the trials as per the admission of the Government of India between 2015 and 2012.

A detailed analysis of unethical practices of drug trials has been reported by Acharya etal.2015.

The problem is drug manufacturers do not declare the full range of possible side effects , and on the trials on minors ,parent's informed consent are not taken to the their full knowledge of side effects. Further, criterion for selecting the target population and many more precautions are ignored.

Genetic and Parental Affinities of Populations

Then,in studies of genetic and parental affinities of populations, many population genetic studies do not take consent of the communities in question while drawing inferences. Therea are many such studies in Indian, but one of the studies on genetic admixture (Kshatriya in 1995), the Sri Lankan Tamil were shown to be closely related to the Sinhalese who were also closely related to Indian Tamils. Kshatriya found the Sri Lankan Tamils to have a greater contribution from the Sinhalese of Sri Lanka (55.20% +/- 9.47) while the Sinhalese had the greatest contribution from South Indian Tamils (69.86% +/- 0.61), followed by Bengalis from the East India (25.41% +/- 0.51). Both the Sri Lankan Tamils and Sinhalese in the island share a common gene pool of 55%. They are farthest from the indigenous Veddahs. This close relationship between the Sri Lankan Tamils and Sinhalese is primarily because they have been close to each other historically, linguistically, and culturally for over 2000 years. Such inferences might contradict the inferences of other scholars and also the indigenous beliefs of the local populations and their indigenous rights.

Such issues raise serious ethical questions related to human rights. UNESCO on human dignity and Human Rights declares: a) Human dignity, human rights and fundamental freedoms are to be fully respected and b) The interests and welfare of the individual have priority over the sole interest of science or society. Similarly, the role of media and civil society and teaching in educational institutions are of utmost important in maintenance of bioethics and human rights. There is therefore, need to strengthen institutional ethical committees and involvement of members of IPs or tribal council in an area of health and bio- medical research, so that they become equal partners and are not exploited culturally, economically, psychologically, biologically and ethically.

References

Acharya, S.K., Das, P.K. and Kshatriya, G.K. 2015. Biomedical research ethics involving humans and issues of human rights. In: Human Rights Education: Issues and Challenges. Ed. By

P. Vatsala. Atlantic Publishers and Distributors, New Delhi. PP 32-48.

Foster. M. and Sharp, R. 2000. Genetic research and culturally specific risks: one size does not fit all. *Trends in Genetics*, 16 (2) : 93-95.

Harmon, A. 2010. *Indian tribe wins fight to limit research of its DNA.* NewYork Timesp. A1.

Hook, R. 2009. "Warrior Genes" the Disease of being Maori. MAI (Maori and Indigenous) Review, 1-11.

ICMR 2017. *National Ethical Guidelines for Bio-medical and Health Research Involving Human Participants.* New Delhi.

Jayaraman, K.S. 2001. Johns Hopkins embroiled in fresh misconduct allegations. *Nature*, 412: 466.

Kowal. E.E. 2015. Genetics and Indigenous communities: Ethical Issues. *International Encyclopedia of the Social & Behavioral Sciences*, 9: 962-966.

Kshatriya, G.K. 1995. Genetic affinities of Sri Lankan populations. *Human Biology*, 67 (6): 843-866.

Minaya, G. and Roque, J. 2015. Ethical problems in Health research with indigenous or originary peoples in Peru. *J. Community Genet*, 6:201-206.

Mudur, G. 2010. Human papilomavirus vaccine project stirs controversy in India. *BMJ*: 340: c1775.

Padma, T.V. 2005. India's drug test. *Nature*, 436: -85 (July).

Rink. H. 1887. *The Eskimo tribes: Their distribution and characteristics, especially in regard to language.* Longman Green & Co, London.

Website

www.who.int/ethics/indigenous_peoples/en/index10...

core.ecu.edu/anth/leibowitzj/2methods.html

http://www.gardasil.com/

CHAPTER – 6

Ethical Issues in Anthropology: Focusing Qualitative Research, Reflexive Method and Field Work

SEKH RAHIM MONDAL

Introduction

In recent times, ethical issues have appeared as very crucial in anthropological research. The most important aspect of anthropological research is its qualitative approach and fieldwork, where the researchers are bound to interact with the human participants. Under such a context, ethical issues have appeared as unavoidable and mandatory on the question of values, rights and dignities of peoples under study.

The present paper is an attempt to highlight the significance of ethical issues in anthropological research and to deal with them the author intends to highlight the need of reflexive method in qualitative research and the ethics in doing fieldwork. The present discourse is based on authors own research and teaching experience in the field of anthropology for more than four decades.

Ethics in Anthropological Research

Ethics in anthropological research indicates the code of conduct, which is nothing but regulatory principles of conducting research on human subjects. Ethical issues are both objective as well as subjective. Ethics are implied on all the stakeholders of research activities. Which is starts from the researchers, research participants, funding agencies and the users of research results. Ethics are primarily associated with the values, principles, intentions and sense of responsibility associated with the study of human subjects. Honesty and morality are the fundamentals of code of conduct. Research ethics are attached with every steps of doing research i.e. both at the level of research design (thinking) and at the level of research proposition (acting). It starts from the very beginning of topic selection up to the end of preparation of research reports (texts) and further from publication of results to its exhibition and use. The first and foremost responsibility of the researcher in anthropology is to ensure and protect the human rights and human dignity of the subjects/peoples under study.

In present context, there is a need of good anthropology for the tough times to save the nature and the peoples, including their societies and cultures. This requires obeying both the subjective as well as the objective ethics. Subjective ethics are associated with anxiety, depression, fear, uncertainty, security, desire, hope and peace of the peoples. All these needs to be reflected in the research design while selecting the topic and theme (proposal) of research. While objective ethics are associated with the ways of the study of peoples which includes methods of field work, nature of data collection, techniques of collecting data, analysis of data, interpretation of data, preparation of report (text or monograph), publication, and use of research results.

For subjective ethical reflections in anthropological studies, there is a need to consider the theoretical and practical implications of countries constitution, laws, governance, planning and policies for its peoples, especially for the folk and indigenous communities. This is very important for problem-oriented research in the discipline to get an insight about what is good and what is bad for the common peoples on whom anthropological studies are mostly carried out.

There is always been a debate between what anthropologists can do as a person and as a professional. This is a crucial ethical question in anthropology. This reminds us the social responsibility of the social or human scientists. The prime social responsibility of the anthropologists is to save the people through their studies and to protect them from the misuse of their research results by the power mongers and profit makers. Research ethics demands minimization of conflict of interests between peoples and professionals. It is to be remembered that many veteran anthropologists of both west and east boldly advocated for people's presence in research for making the world safe for peoples in general and indigenous and marginal communities in particular for peaceful living of common peoples.

It is also argued by many that anthropological researches today need to be oriented to words human (social) and national development by bridging the gap between theoretical, applied and action researches for the sake of peoples and the country as well. Therefore, anthropological research should not be confined only in the domain of knowledge production but also to think how the knowledge be utilized. In this context the role of anthropological (professional) organizations and associations have a very crucial role to play. However, unfortunately their roles are primarily confined to organize seminars and conferences rather than to make a bridge between professionals and policy makers.

It is very difficult to ignore that the discipline of anthropology still bearing colonial, neo-colonial and neo-traditional heritage. It is usually blamed that, most of the anthropological studies are directly or indirectly used by the rulers and administrators to govern and control the peoples for their political and vested interest. To combat such a notion there is an urgent need to follow the ethical guidelines of conducting anthropological research for the benefit of the common peoples. (Ahmed and Shore: 1995, Bourdieu: 1992, Foucault: 1980).

Reflexivity and Ethics in Qualitative Research

Reflexivity in qualitative research is now an emerging method of anthropological enquiry. Qualitative approach primarily deals with the empirical aspects on special characteristics of a particular group. As a method, it starts with the fieldwork from the perspectives and actions of the peoples (participants) under study. Qualitative research primarily guided by positivistic approach, thus deals more with the objective facts of overt or explicit human behavior, where the covert or implicit i.e. people's subjective aspects are not much taken into consideration. Ethical issue sunder such an anthropological enquiry thus obviously a great question. To fill up this gap, reflexivity as a method of critical social enquiry has appeared as an essential component in qualitative and ethnographic research. It provides the perspectives for successful exploration and interpretation of field data (biological, social, cultural, psychological) on human subjects for drawing logical conclusion.

Ethics in anthropological research demands reflexivity, which involves reflection at several steps of doing research and for several themes. It gives the researcher a direction for self-correction including the morals and values to situate and activate the holistic research process for knowledge production and beyond i.e. utilization of results for the benefit of the people. There are varieties of reflexivity already exists in anthropology. The most important of them are new-ethnography, ethno-methodology etc. Reflexive method advocates for "emic" and insider perspective in qualitative ethnography, which is fundamentally guided by "cultural relativity". This requires open dialogue between the researchers with the research participants. All these we learn from classroom lectures and books, but unfortunately, its practice is still not much reflected neither in ethnographic research nor in production of text. This is a great limitation in anthropological research on ethical ground.

Reflexivity helps the researcher to draw the relationship between the processes of knowledge production with the involvement of the knowledge producer. Reflexivity in the context of researcher's ethics constantly assess the relationship between knowledge production, ways of producing knowledge and power as well as motives behind such endeavors. Reflexivity clearly suggests that the researcher should pay a serious attention to know the ways that how different linguistic, social, cultural, political, philosophical, theoretical and even biological elements are linked together in the entire research process. Actually, the researcher in anthropology is usually unaware about utilization of their research results. They even do not know whether their research is used for good or bad for the concerned people. This is one unresolved issue and ethical question in anthropology.

In reflexive ethnographic research interpretation and explanation comes to the forefront of research activities, which calls for awareness about necessity of sound theoretical knowledge, appropriate methodology, logical paradigm and enormous empirical facts. Actually, all these constitutes the major determinants of interpretation of social behavior and culture. The idea is that the facts, observations, and statements of interviewed subjects including the facts obtained from secondary sources all have relationship to "something" or anything, which needs to be explored and highlighted on ethical ground.

Another element of reflection is to question the topics of research, peoples and societies targeted for research, including the intellectual traditions governed by power and funding agencies. Reflexivity is the self-appraisal and self-corrections of one's own research in true ethical sense. This may help in interpretation of empirical material including their relevance and representation.

Dialog based on ethically second guidelines are now considered as essential components of postmodern reflexive ethnography. This opens the door of walking and on fond ethnography. The individuals as members of a social/cultural group inhabit and exhibit their life ways under specific environmental, social and cultural contexts. This requires detailed description and analysis of empirical facts on place, people, materiality, perception, feeling and bindings. The bridging between the subjective position of researcher and subjective structure of peoples under study is very necessary in anthropological fieldwork under changing context. This requires varied forms of walking on the part of researcher, which starts from physical walking to the field i.e. (place and people) and then move towards the fields of their social, cultural and psychological domains. This is important as the field sites in anthropology are day by day turning towards virtual sites.

Ethically sound reflexive methodology also questions the conventional anthropological concepts of tribe, society, culture, village, community; including family, marriage etc. as those have lost some of their basic elements and acquired new characteristics under present situation. Therefore, review and reform of many of the anthropological concepts are very necessary for proper and fruitful research. Reflexivity helps in philosophical and ethical reflections in respect to researcher assumption, examination, interaction and interpretation of empirical material. (Ahmed and Shore: 1995, Bourdieu and Wacquant: 1992, Foucult: 1980, Maranho: 1991).

Ethics in Field Work

The most important aspect of anthropological research is its method of doing fieldwork and collection of first-hand data. In fieldwork, a researcher is bound to interact with the varieties of peoples having varied life ways. In fieldwork the ethics, i.e. code of conduct is very crucial. Unfortunately, ethical issues are relatively low in fieldwork. This is due to the historical growth of the discipline and motives behind anthropological studies of "other culture". The colonial and postcolonial legacy actually shaped the conventional field studies, and which has made the anthropologists as data hungry persons without considering their relevance and representation. This is a serious ethical question on the ground of human rights of the peoples under study. Ethics is usually concerned as problematic in anthropological fieldwork, as its prime goal is to gather data; particularly from folk, indigenous, marginal and power less peoples or communities to help the rulers, administrators and so-called development experts.

In recent times due to awareness about ontology, epistemology and reflexivity in methodology of anthropological research, the ethical issues have come forward in field studies. Ethics in fieldwork is very essential for the emergence of the significance of human rights, indigenous rights, gender rights and self-esteem of human subjects.

Ethics are primarily associated with the three major steps of doing fieldwork. The first step, is the background of research which including problem identification, formulation of research design, selection of peoples to be studies and places where field work to be conducted. Research objectives should be transparent. The second stage is to know the laws associated with the place and people, which means legal restrictions and code of conduct for working with the targeted groups, as well as the place where they live in. In this context researcher must obey and follow the manners associated with the study of "others", particularly the marginal, vulnerable, stigmatized and sensitive groups. The third step is the actual fieldwork. This is the most innovative part of conducting field research without causing any harm of the peoples and their cultures. The most common lesson in this context is to live with the people or in close proximity, and use the local assistants and interpreters to learn the manners and customs of the local population. This is necessary for establishing good rapport and impression for the sake of data to day interaction and data collection. Fieldwork to be conducted slowly but gradually by convincing the people about the goal of data collection for each other benefit, direct or indirect. Anthropologists usually follow the "participant observer" or 'observer participant" method for conducting field work. Ethical issues in this context are how far in real sense it is "participant"? Actually, anthropologists are getting direct benefit out of their fieldwork, but their research participants are far away from its direct benefit. Hence, anthropologists should give priority to take up such studies with which people will be benefited in due course.

In anthropological fieldwork the role of informants and respondents are highly significant, without their help and participation, fieldwork is practically impossible. Ethics here to give them credit and proper recognition nor simply by acknowledging them but by considering and crediting them as "research partner". It is the duty of the anthropologists to give proper appreciation to their informants or respondents as their partner of research while producing the texts and reports. Success of fieldwork depends on depth of data collection and for which rapport establishment with the research participants or partners is very important following the cultural norms of the people. Seeking consent for data collection and maintaining confidentiality of field data are the most vital aspects of ethics.

The first and foremost responsibility of a field worker is to ensure rights and dignities of peoples under study. Fieldwork is the most reliable source of first-hand data collection and it is an essential component of anthropological research. In fieldwork, interaction between researcher and people (group or community) is very essential. In the ways of interaction, there are chances of both good and bad effects, either on the part of researcher or on community. Since researcher require data, so accountability comes to his/her shoulder. In the process of interaction ethical code of conduct to be followed by the researcher to make the interaction fruitful and peaceful without causing any harm.

Survey research is also now played are important role in anthropology, particularly for the sake of planning and policymaking. In survey, research schedules and questionnaires are used as tools. Therefore, ethical issues are also important in designing and framing of tools of research. The researcher should follow the code of conduct to ask necessary questions to a respondent. It is the researcher's duty to follow the modest manner in framing and asking question, so that participants should not have feeling that those are asked to them in authoritative manner. It is to be remember that methodology of data collection is important as important the quality of data for credibility of research.

For fieldwork researcher's own identity playing a very crucial role. This has learned from my own field experience. Being myself as a Muslim, have faced several awkward questions and even critical/tough situations while conducting field work among both Muslim and non-Muslim groups (population) viz. tribes, castes and other socio-religious communities. Being a male scholar, I have also faced problems while working on women's issues. I realized that, ethically or morally guided impression management and rapport establishment is the only way to handle the critical field situation. It is necessary for a field worker to transcend his/her social identity to an identity of a researcher free from bias and prejudices of all forms.

Ethical issues differ in different field situation. It varies from context to context, people to people, and society to society. It varies in terms of age, gender and social status of the persons under research. Ethical issues even different for different types of research i.e. exploratory research, problem-oriented research and diagnostic research etc. It is very true that field work is very tough and sensitive in the case of the study of indigenous communities. In this context the most important lesson is that fieldwork as a learning process, it is to be learned simply by doing fieldwork, following the norms of honesty, morality and accountability. Honesty is the most important quality of ethics in fieldwork. Field worker must aware about ethical responsibility of collecting data, interpretation of data and production and publication of texts based on field data.

There are number of international anthropological professional organizations those have already prescribed the ethical guide lines to the researchers. In India ICMR and many other research organizations have also prescribed the ethical guidelines. Nevertheless, it is also to be considered that no code is unique but depends on contexts, circumstances and situations. Hence it is the duty of a field worker to follow the prescribed guidelines whatever available and evolve the guidelines of owns own for the sake of his/her field studies. (Alvesson and Skoldberg: 2000, Miller and Dingwall: 1997, Giddens: 1976, Mondal: 2012, Silverman: 1985, Sinha: 1978, Srivastava: 2004).

Concluding Remarks

The concern of contemporary anthropology is to produce research, which is ethically sound. It is to be ensured that research should help not only to know the people, their biology and culture, but also to protect and develop them if require. Reflexivity is now appeared as a powerful method in qualitative and ethnographic research. It includes reflections at all steps of doing research and ethical issues involved with all of them. It is the duty of the researchers to follow the codes of conduct while doing their respective research. Reflexive methodology explicitly advocated for ethically sound research methods and techniques for doing empirical field-based research.

While collecting data from our informant or respondent we have to think (a) are they for our data, (b) are they for our degree, (c) are they for our research project. (d) why they give us data and (e) what they will get out of data giving to us? Therefore, we have to think on all those issues and alike questions. Since we need data for the sake of our professional necessity, we have to gather them through ethically sound code of conduct and with much caution. We have to remember that our informants or respondents are our research partners, so we have to behave and interact with them accordingly as the partners.

References

Ahmed Akbar and C. Shore, 1995. *The Future of Anthropology*, London: Athlone.

Alvesson Mats and Skoldberg Kaj, 2000. *Reflexive Methodology: A New Vista for Qualitative Research*, London: Sage Publications.

Bourdieu ,P and Wacquant, L.J.D., 1992. *An Invitation to Reflexive Sociology*, Cambridge: Policy Press.

Faucault, M. 1980. *Power / Knowledge*, New York, Pantheon.

Gidden. A, 1976. *New Rules of Sociological Method: A Positive Critique of Interpretative Sociologies*, London: Hutchinson.

Miller, G and Diangwall, R. 1997. *Context and Method of Qualitative Research*, London, Sage Publication.

Mondal, Sekh Rahim, 2012. "Reflexive Method in Qualitative Research : An Introduction, in *Himalayan Miscellany*, Vol. 23, pp 1-3.

Maranho, T. 1991. "Reflexion, Dialogue and the Subject", in F. Steir (Ed)., *Research and Reflexivity*, London; Sage Publication.

Srivastava, V.K. (Ed.), 2004. *Methodology and Field Work*, New Delhi: Oxford University Press.

Sinha, S.C. (Ed.), 1978. *Field Studies on the People of India*, Calcutta: The Indian Anthropological Society.

Silverman, D., 1985. *Qualitative Methodology in Sociology*, Alder Shot: Gower.

CHAPTER – 7

Ethical Issues in Fieldwork: Traditional versus Modern Approach

MONIKA SAINI AND A. K. KAPOOR

Introduction

"Ethics is the study of the principles and standards of human conduct" (Pettifor, 1996). Ethics can be considered as a method, procedure or perspective for determining how to act for analysing complex problems or issues. In general sense, ethics are the norms of conduct that differentiate between right and wrong behaviour.

Various institutions and disciplines issue norms or guidelines for proper conduct of the behaviour to meet their particular aims and objectives. For instance, medicine, law, engineering, and business sectors have their own ethical standards or norms of conduct that differentiates between acceptable and non-acceptable behaviours. These norms also govern members of the associated discipline to coordinate their activities and to build the trust of the discipline with the public. Ethical norms are also applicable to the people who conduct scientific research or other scholarly activities. These scientific activities are governed by a specialized discipline, research ethics, which studies and maintains the standards of the conduct.

The following section underlines the importance of ethnical norms in research:

- Ethical norms actively promote the prime aims of a research i.e. increase in knowledge, validation of assumptions and avoidance of error.

- Ethical standards and norms encourage the morals and values required to do essential collaborative research work. These morals and values include mutual respect, trust and accountability, and fairness which form the basis of cooperation and coordination among researchers from different background and institutions.

- Ethical norms help to ensure the accountability of the research and researchers to the public which helps to get funding for the large-scale research projects. Good quality research work is more likely to receive funding from the external sources.

- Lastly, many of the ethical norms promote a variety of social values, such as social responsibility, human rights, environmental protection, animal welfare, compliance with the law, and health and safety (Resnik, 2011).

Research Ethics and Guidelines

The ethics of research has been significantly complicated over the last several decades as a consequence of the "interpretive turn" (shift from quantitative and deductive methods to theoretical and inductive methods) and the ever-increasing use of qualitative research methods that have accompanied it (Howe and Moses, 1999). Before outlining the ethical issues of fieldwork, a concise description of the ethical principles and standards is presented below.

Ethical Issues in Fieldwork   89

The first guidebook for ethical research and practice was developed by the American Psychological Association (APA) in 1953. Over the years, several regulations were proposed in order to accompany the researchers in their activities. In 2002, American Anthropological Association proposed five principles for the research ethics.

1. **Beneficence and Nonmaleficence:** Researchers are responsible for the well-being of those they work with, either human or animal. They must do not harm or try to minimize the negative consequence of their actions in those situations where conflicts arise between their obligations. Also, professionals must control their religious, political or financial interests in order not to interfere with their clients.

2. **Fidelity and Responsibility:** Researchers are responsible for their clients, their colleagues and the society. They uphold the professional standards, accept responsibility for their behaviour and cooperate with other professionals when needed.

3. **Integrity:** Researchers are honest and truthful about their work. When deception is ethically justifiable to maximize the benefits and minimize the harms, the professionals must minimize any negative effect of the technique they have used.

4. **Justice:** Every person has the right to benefit from the results of research and practice. Also, researchers must adhere to unbiased techniques and recognize the limitations of their competence in offering their clients the best service available.

5. **Respect for People's Rights and Dignity:** This principle reinforces the obligation to be aware and

respectful towards cultural and individual diversity. Researchers must not be biased towards religion, gender, age, race, culture, sexual orientation, disability or socio-economic status. Also, they must offer equal services to everyone in need, regardless of their different status (Turliuc and Candel, 2019).

As the present study discusses the ethical issues under the realm of anthropological research (study of humankind in all its aspects), only those ethical guidelines which relate to human subjects have been presented. Summarized below are the ethical guidelines for research with human subjects, which were published in 1981 by American Psychological Association. These regulations have been incorporated into broader ethical guidelines which can be found on the APA website (www.apa.org).

- In planning research, a researcher or an investigator is held responsible for evaluating and ensuring the ethical acceptability. Researcher must obtain ethical advice when needed and must apply required safeguards to protect the rights of the participants.

- Investigator must ensure that all the researchers, collaborators, assistants, employees associated with a research project are following the ethical norms and standards.

- Investigator must obtain the informed consent from all the participants prior to the research. In case of children, consent must be obtained from their parent or any other responsible surrogate.

- Investigator must fully respect the decision of the participants' to decline or withdraw his/her participation at any given point of time.

- Investigator must ensure the safety and protection of the participants from any kind of physical or mental harm arising from the research procedure and methodology.

- After collection of data, the investigator must also provide the suitable ways to contact him/her if the participant(s) ask for any disclosure, explanation clarification and answer.

- Researcher is also responsible to detect and remove any short-term or long-term negative effects and consequences of the research.

- All information obtained must be held in confidentiality (Graziano and Raulin, 2012).

Many academic books and articles present ethical considerations as a single-standing compartmentalized section without giving much importance. However, in actual scenario, ethical issues coincide with every aspect of research process. The present study describes ethical issues in relation to a particular aspect of research, i.e. fieldwork and delineates the distinction between traditional and modern approaches of fieldwork. The article also highlights the ethical dilemmas of anthropological fieldwork.

Traditional Versus Modern Fieldwork

In qualitative studies, fieldwork is often used as a method of engaging with the phenomenon to gather information/ data or to analyze practices in situ. Fieldwork, as a specific intervention practice, is work done in the field, close to people. In traditional anthropology, the field comprised a geographical, physical boundary, defined by the object of study, which was typically a tribe or tribal unit. The researcher entered the field physically with the expressed aim of getting closer to the unknown "other." The process is embodied and active, requiring both mundane and significant adjustments on the part of the ethnographer in terms of dress, manner, language, and other elements of embodiment that might convey a message. Close attention to these details would be an initial step in successfully navigating through the first, most obvious set of boundaries. Furthermore, the active positioning of the investigator in the form of participant observer is the hallmark of anthropological and ethnographic inquiry. In fact, participant observation is and was often interchangeable with the term "fieldwork" in traditional anthropological training. First hand relations with those studied provides valuable means to get closer to their understanding of their own everyday lives. Collecting "naturally occurring" discourse was accomplished traditionally by listening and then later recalling in writing what was said, when, and to whom (Markham, 2013).

Apart from the instrumental aspects of fieldwork-the field, participant observation, observation and participation, many more significant tools and techniques are also embedded in the traditional anthropological fieldwork. These tools and techniques consist of interviewing, field writings, photography and sketching and collection of artifacts from the local settings. According to Geertz (1973), writing field notes engage the researcher in a process of cultural inscription. This process of selecting from the context and then writing it elsewhere simultaneously abstracts from lived experiences and restricts attention to a particular aspect that will be read textually.

In the past few decades, emerging technologies have transformed the anthropological fieldwork practices. Digital and social media- that is, social networking sites (Facebook, MySpace, LinkedIn), blogs, "microblogging" services (Twitter, Tumblr), and media sharing platforms (YouTube, Flickr, Instagram) and mobile networking, especially on internet enabled mobile phones are remaking anthropological understanding of the field, fieldwork and field notes. Field notes serve to make the field a certain kind of place. Social and mobile media are remaking these practices in multiple ways, providing new platforms and formats for creating field materials and brining relationships and interactions from different parts of life into closer proximity (Sanjek and Tratner, 2016).

On one hand, the engagement of researcher with participants through digital and social media technologies yield significant benefits in the form of sampling, data collection and analysis while on the other hand also pose many challenges and compromises to the traditional anthropological practices. For instance, the observational method of fieldwork often adopts the form of archiving on social media platforms where researchers learn from the "virtual data" rather than through sustained engagement in the natural settings.

Ethical Issues in Fieldwork

The embedded distinction between traditional and modern approaches of fieldwork creates many ethical issues. Some of the major ethical issues are presented below:

- **Informed Consent:** The increasing virtual interaction between researcher and participants through social media brings up the important ethical issue of "informed consent". Getting an informed consent from the participant, either verbal or written is an essential part of the research work. Making friends on social networking sites like Facebook and gaining information in relation to the research work does not legitimize a researcher to assume that an informed consent has been obtained.

- **Biasness:** Virtual interaction with the participants via social networking websites also makes researcher's personal credentials or information accessible to the public. Participants make perceptions about the researcher on the basis of their civil status, religious and political views which are available on the researcher's social networking page. For example, a certain section of people who are associated with a particular group may refuse to participate in a research project which seems different from their ideologies and views. This can eventually create biasness in the selection of the research sample.

- **Anonymity:** Engaging with participants through social networking websites is generally considered as an acknowledgement that the particular person has agreed to take part in the research project which ultimately affects the participant's anonymity. This particularly affects when the number of participants are less in a given location or setting. In this scenario, it becomes easier to trace any given information provided by a particular respondent.

- **Privacy and Confidentiality:** Virtual fieldwork also compromise with the confidentiality of the data provided by the respondent. Social networking websites are regarded as public space as they are publicly accessible. Maintaining privacy and confidentiality on internet websites is extremely difficult and pose severe challenge to the ethical principle of "no harm to the participant".

Anthropological Fieldwork and Ethical Dilemma

Anthropological research is different from other social science researches. Unlike sociologists and psychologists who work in complex societies and often conduct surveys and experiments with the clients, anthropologists being field scientists, learn from their informants. Anthropologists are very well known for their field work methods and approaches.

However, while conducting fieldwork, investigators have comparatively little power over those who are studied: informants are usually free to leave the situation or to decline to enter interaction. Subjects control the setting of research and influence the context, with interaction flowing comparatively freely in both directions. Nevertheless, variations do exist within fieldwork, and they can be measured along the same dimensions used for the other modes of research. At one extreme where the fieldworker sits in some government office and subjects are brought to the office of the researcher for questioning about the customs and jargon of their fellows. Such fieldwork is characterized by the relatively high perceived power and authoritativeness of ethnographers, and a somewhat one-sided interaction flowing from investigators toward those studied. This form of fieldwork might be considered ethically questionable, even if subjects suffer little or no harm and the research benefits human knowledge. Here, investigator destroys the independence of subjects by means of coercion, thus violating the ethical principles of autonomy. On the other hand, the researcher tries in every conceivable fashion by going native and adopts the way of life of the common people being studied while also conducting research and maintaining filed notes. Here, the investigator has little or no relative power of the context of research, and interaction flows in two directions. In this type of fieldwork, however, the fact that an interaction or procedure would result in few harm would not be sufficient to have it judged ethically adequate. In making such judgements, it is more the quality of the interaction than the results that must be scrutinized (Cassell, 1980).

Summary

Ethical issues in the field of anthropological research are majorly dependent on the conduct of individual researchers rather than the ethical norms asserted by the professional bodies. Ethical standards only assist traditional and modern anthropological fieldworkers to reach an unbiased and satisfactory resolution of their research conflicts. These guidelines serve to educate and sensitize anthropologists about the potential sources of ethical dilemmas arising in the process of research. Virtual fieldwork is susceptible to many ethical risks but if these risks ae carefully managed, fieldwork process may benefit tremendously from these communication technologies. On the basis of the foresightedness and informed deliberation, the researcher should contemplate the departure from the ethical standards and must ensure the where the privileging of concerned group(s) is ethically necessary. The researcher who does the fieldwork should also examine the ethical dilemmas particular to the type of research. He/she should discover the appropriate ethical principles and must develop the skills to apply them in the best ways.

References

Cassell, J. 1980. Ethical Principles for Conducting Fieldwork. *American anthropologist*, *82*(1), 28-41.

Geertz, C. 1973. *The Interpretation of Cultures: Selected essays*. New York: Basic Books.

Graziano, A. M., & Raulin, M. L. 2012. APA Ethical Guidelines for Research with Human Subjects. *Research Methods: A Process of Inquiry* (8th ed.) Pearson.

Howe, K. R., & Moses, M. S. 1999. Chapter 2: Ethics in Educational Research. *Review of research in education*, *24*(1), 21-59.

Markham, A. N. 2013. Fieldwork in social media: What would Malinowski do?. *Qualitative Communication Research*, *2*(4), 434-446.

Pettifor, J. L. 1996. Ethics: Virtue and Politics in the Science and Practice of Psychology. *Canadian Psychology/Psychologie canadienne*, *37*(1), 1.

Resnik, D. B. 2011. What is Ethics in Research & Why is it Important. *National Institute of Environmental Health Sciences*, *1*(10), 49-70. Retrieved from https://www.veronaschools.org/cms/lib02/NJ01001379/Centricity/Domain/588/What%20is%20Ethics%20in%20Research%20Why%20is%20it%20Important.pdf

Sanjek, R., & Tratner, S. W. (Eds.). 2016. *eFieldnotes: The makings of anthropology in the digital world*. University of Pennsylvania Press.

Turliuc, M. N., & Candel, O. S. 2019. Ethical Issues in Couple and Family Research and Therapy. In *Ethics in Research Practice and Innovation* (pp. 226-242). IGI Global.

CHAPTER – 8

Ethical issues in Anthropological Research: Participant Observation

SUBIR BISWAS

Introduction

Ethical or specifically bioethical issues in respect of participant observation is utmost important and unique in the sense that here researcher supposed to participate in some aspects of life around them and record it accordingly. In other words, the observer (researcher) takes part in the situation being studied while carrying out his/ her research. The history of participant observation in anthropology is old but still significant. Malinowski's (1922) work among the Trobriand Islanders is one of the earliest evidences of use of participant observation as a method of data collection. In anthropology, the term participant observation is more or less synonymous with living in a remote/ tribal village learning the ways of their exotic culture of the people. But Guest el al (2013) opined that "Many participant observation studies are not as lengthy in duration as ethnography, are less comprehensive in scope, and are conducted in relatively mundane locations. But even when it is used on a limited basis, there is no denying the power of this technique to produce penetrating insights and highly contextual understanding".

According to Guest *et al.* (2013) the basic bioethical elements of Participants observation are-(i) Getting into the location of whatever aspect of the human experience you wish to study, (ii) Building rapport with the participants, and (iii) Spending enough time interacting to get the needed data.

How to obtain Inform consent?

The main issue of bioethics which is very much related with Participant observation method is informed/ voluntary consent- by which research participants after assessing risk-benefit was well as confidentiality of the research will agree to participate and will allow the observer (researcher) to observe the situation. Therefore, it includes the issue of transparency or what the research is about and what is the ultimate aim of the research; the issue of confidentiality by which researcher will guaranty that informants contribution and information will not be disclosed without informant's consent. And last but not the least, as stated earlier observer should disclose the risk of the participant because of participating in the study. In some cases, compensation because of the time spends by the participants for the sake of research also highlighted, especially when it is a funded research.

The next question that may come to our mind in respect of informed consent is- from whom should consent be taken? Is it leaders or gatekeepers or all of the participants who are supposed to be observed by the observer?" If we consider inform consent from all the participants, there is a risk of altering natural behaviour by the participants. In all cases, consent will initially be sought from leaders or gatekeepers of the society/ group. However, it is the duty of the observer to introduce and identify him/ herself as a researcher/ observer to all, even when it is a large heterogeneous group. By this, I am not arguing for introducing to all the participants, rather the researcher takes practicable steps to be recognised by the local community for what he/she is. In this context, we can quote the statement by American Sociological Association (1999) "Many of those participating in public events observed by the anthropologist will not be known to him or her. This is particularly the case for strangers visiting the community (a term that could also include employees of government agencies, multinational corporations, schools, hospitals among others) being studied; or in research on mobile groups (which could involve pastoral and nomadic groups, refugees or expatriate and corporate elites) who move around for various reasons (such as subsistence, ritual celebrations, pilgrimage, corporate meetings, wartime displacements) to other places; or in studies of large institutions. In such situations, the anthropologists should take all practicable steps to be introduced by local participants and identify him/herself as a researcher".

There supposed to be various ethical and legal questions to use covert research methods, because covert research violates basic principles of informed consent as well as privacy of the participants. Therefore, it is only permissible when no other method is useful to obtain essential data. In this context Statement of Ethical Practice for the British Sociological Association (March 2002) stated that "In such studies it is important to safeguard the anonymity of research participants. Ideally, where informed consent has not been obtained prior to the research it should be obtained post-hoc". However, American Sociological Association (1999) waived informed consent in respect to observation in public places or other settings where no rules of privacy are provided by law or custom.

Ethical issues in Anthropological Research   101

Is IRB approval required?

Participant observation method involves naturalistic behavior of a group or society; we thought that the question of review by Institutional Review Board (IRB) may not arise. But according to American Anthropological Association code of ethics (1998) review by an Institutional Review Board is essential to ensure "that the participants in the proposed research are not harmed. Because of its complexity, variable contexts, and duration of different ethnographic research projects, ethnographic research should be reviewed on a case-by-case basis". Generally, in natural setting research the magnitude of harm such as uncertainty, embracement, and boredom are usually low, but in many cases the possible magnitude of harm could be high; and IRB should consider social and cultural harm also instead of physical, psychological, political or economic harm of the group. Associations of Social Anthropologists of the UK and Commonwealth (2011) also opined that "Participants should be made aware of the presence and purpose of the researcher whenever reasonably practicable. Researchers should inform participants of their research in the most appropriate way depending on the context of the research".

How will individuals' privacy/ confidentiality be protected?

Now, one can worried about confidentiality of his/ her information. Even some of the evidences that observer collected during his/her stay can lead to social/ economic/ political or physical harm of the informants; or even judicial punishment. According to Kapoor (2014) "the obligation to protect research participants' anonymity and keep research data in confidence is an all-inclusive one and should be fulfilled specific arrangements to the contrary are made

102 *Research Ethics, Indigenous Communities and Fieldwork*

by the participants themselves". Therefore, it is the duty of the observer not to disclose such issues publicly, even the researcher supposed to relinquish the data that may identify the members directly or indirectly. In this context, Rabinowitz (2016) opined that *"No one but the individual working with a particular participant will have access to information about or records of that participant without her permission. At this level of confidentiality, records and notes are usually kept under lock and key, and computer records should be protected by electronic coding or passwords".*

Taking field notes in field condition also requires ethical dimension of its own. Field notes of the observer are mainly personal and barring any kind of legal exceptions. However, in such cases confidentiality and anonymity of the participants should be ensured. It is the duty of the observer to protect notes from any kind of unauthorized access. According to Kawulich (2005) "ethical responsibility is to preserve the anonymity of the participants in the final write-up and in field notes to prevent their identification, should the field notes be subpoenaed for inspection. Individual identities must be described in ways that community members will not be able to identify the participants".

Photographs or filming may be considered as important tool for participant observation, and also requires lots of ethical considerations. When photographing, you supposed to ask their permission first. However, sometimes prior permission is not possible; is such cases ask permission after photographing/ filming.

Is there any conflict of interest?

Conflict of interest, like other type of research, also plays an important role in participant observation. It is such a situation in which personal or financial considerations have the potential to influence findings of the research. One criticism that has caused discomfort in respect of today's participant observation is probably the way their project is funded for the interest of funders. Financial relationship can create conflict of interest between researcher's ethical/ scientific obligations and funder's desire for financial or other gain. Several studies have identified such situation where results benefiting sponsors by manipulating results, preparing poor study design, and withholding negative data for publications.

American Speech-Language Hearing Association's (2016) recommendation in this regard is simple and three folds- *avoid, disclose*, or recuse. The best thing to do is probably to avoid such situations that can lead to conflict of interest. This does not mean that you have to avoid funding agency, but there should be no conflict of interest between funders and ethical obligations. The second thing is to disclose is to IRB and even your participants, if there is any sort of conflict of interest. And lastly, recuse him or her, from the study because of a conflict of interest.

The question of relationship

Last, but not least, which is very much important and unique in case of participant observation is relationship established by the observer with his/ her participants. The researcher, in course of observation has to establish and maintain a close relationship to obtain qualitative data. This close contact and dependences require even more ethical practices other than present day norms of bioethics (Biswas, 2015). One of the main important aspects of such rapport is to speak the language of the people you are studying. The researcher

104 *Research Ethics, Indigenous Communities and Fieldwork*

supposed to stay a long time, possibly within the group to establish friendship or rapport, some of which can extend over lifetime, but unfortunately many of them ended with research. The relation one supposed to establish can help further observation/ research by the same researcher or even others.

Concluding Remarks

Participants observation, because of its uniqueness in respect of observer and observe direct interaction over time may encounter with lots of ethical enquiries which supposed to overcome mostly by observer. Generally, the research alone supposed to stay with his/ her participants in a strange situation. Shah (2006) opined that "in the case of participant observation the ethical problems are faced usually by only the individual researcher. In the case of survey research, on the other hand, a team of researchers would face such problems. These problems multiply with the increasing size of the survey, culminating in nationwide surveys and censuses."

And last, but not the least, in such a strange situation, where no one is there to help you other than your participants, you have to explore your own code of ethics which may differ ethical code of conduct as enacted by others. There is no universal solution to ethical consideration in respect of different ethnic groups or even individuals within a group. Say, for example, all of the western association argued for 'written consent', even if your research is observational/ non-experimental; but one can understand difficulties of having written consent from non-literate (even can sign group) tribal even village or urban population of India. However, that does not mean your intrusion without consent, but you may have 'verbal consent' (or use of voice recorder, if the risk is not less than minimal) after elaborating your objectives, risk-benefit and so on.

Indian context, on the other hand, exhibits different norms to encounter ethical dilemmas, which may differ from Western bioethics. Even different parts of India may not follow same rule of action. Field work or participant observation among two groups residing nearby are not similar. Therefore, to establish ethical code for field work in respect of Indian context is utmost important.

References

AAA 1998. *Code of Ethics of the American Anthropological Association*, Arlington, American Anthropological Association.

American Speech-Language Hearing Association 2016. *Issues in Ethics: Conflicts of Professional Interest*, http://www.asha.org/ Practice/ethics/Conflicts-of-Professional-Interest/ Accessed on March 7, 2019.

ASA 1999. *Code of Ethics*, Washington, American Sociological Association.

ASA 2011. *ASA Ethical Guidelines*, London, Associations of Social Anthropologists of the UK and Commonwealth.

Biswas S. 2015. Ethics in Anthropological Research: Responsibilities to the Participants. *Human Biology Review* 4(3), 250-263.

BSA 2002. *Statement of Ethical Practice for the British Sociological Association*, Belmont, British Sociological Association.

Guest, G, Namey EE and Mitchell, ML 2013. *Collecting Qualitative Data: A Field Manual for Applied Research*, New Delhi, Sage Publication.

Kapoor AK. 2014. Ethical Issues and Perspectives. In: Ethical Issues in Anthropological Research. ed by Subir Biswas, pp.1-15. Delhi: Concept Publishing Co, Delhi.

Kawulich, BB 2005. Participant Observation as a Data Collection Method, *Forum: Qualitative Social Research* 6(2): Art 43.

Malinowski, B 1922. *Argonauts of the Western Pacific: An account of native enterprise and adventure in the Archipelagoes of Melanesian New Guinea. London, Routledge and Kegan Paul*

Rabinowitz, Phil 2016. *Ethical Issues in Community Interventions,* http://ctb.ku.edu/en/table-of-contents/analyze/choose-and-adapt-community-interventions/ethical-issues/main, Accessed on March 7, 2019.

Shah, AM 2006. *Ethics in Sociological and Social Anthropological Research: A Brief Note,* eSS Co

CHAPTER – 9

GREATS - Guidelines for Research Ethics in Anthropological Studies: An Appraisal

MITHUN DAS

Ethics means the discipline dealing with what is good and bad and with moral duty and obligation (Merriam-Webster 2020). In other words, the moral principles that govern a person's behaviour while conducting any activity. According to World Health Organization (WHO), Research Ethics govern the standards of conduct for scientific researchers. It is important to adhere to ethical principles in order to protect the rights, welfare and dignity of the research participants. All research involving human beings should be reviewed by an ethics committee to ensure that the appropriate ethical standards are being upheld. Discussion of the ethical principles of beneficence, justice and autonomy are central to ethical review (Nuremberg Code 1947).

History of research Ethics goes back to the **Nuremberg Code** in 1947. It is the most important document in the history of the ethics of medical research. It was formulated in 1947 in Nuremberg, Germany, by American judges sitting in judgment of Nazi doctors accused of conducting murderous and torturous human experiments in the concentration camp (Declaration of Helsinki. 1964). In code it was mentioned that:

1. It is of utmost importance to obtain voluntary consent of the research participant. This means that the person involved should have legal capacity to give consent; should be so situated as to be able to exercise free power of choice, without the intervention of any element of force, fraud, deceit, duress, over-reaching, or other ulterior form of constraint or coercion; and should have sufficient knowledge and comprehension of the elements of the subject matter involved, as to enable him to make an understanding and enlightened decision.

2. The research experiment should be done in such a way as to yield fruitful results for the betterment of the society, which is otherwise unprocurable by other methods or means of study, and hence not be random and unnecessary in nature.

3. The research should be so designed and based on the results of experimentation and knowledge of the natural history of the disease or other problem considered in the study, that the expected results would justify the performance of the research findings, i.e., the functional output of the research.

4. The research should be conducted in such a way that one could avoid all unnecessary physical and mental suffering including injury.

5. No research should be conducted, if there is an *a priori* reason of having any chance that death or disabling injury would occur; excepting in those research where the experimental physicians also serve as research participants.

6. The degree of risk should be taken in to account seriously by keeping in mind that it must not exceed

that determined by the humanitarian importance, whatsoever and howsoever, of the problem to be solved by the concerned researcher(s).

7. Adequate facilities must be provided and necessary preparations must be taken in order to protect the research participants from any remote possibilities of disability, or death, and even chances of injury during the research work.

8. The experiment part of the research should be conducted by the scientifically qualified persons only.

9. During the entire course of the research work, the research participant should have the liberty to quite at any time for reason whatsoever and howsoever.

10. Similarly during the entire course of the research work, the scientist/investigator must be prepared to terminate the research at any stage, if one has probable cause to believe, keeping the food faith, that superior skill and careful judgment is required of him, and that the continuation of the work is likely to result in injury, disability, or death to the concerned research participant.

It is however reasonable to mention that the Nuremberg code is incomplete to some degree but, it served as a blueprint for the present available principles that ensure rights of subjects. After that it was the World Medical Association **Declaration of Helsinki** (1964) which became a remarkable document for medical doctors to safeguard the health of the people. Both the Nuremberg Code and the Declaration of Helsinki served as models for various research regulations across the globe, which require not only informed consent of the research participant, but also prior review of the research proposals by a committee like Institutional Review Boards of

USA following Federal regulations, and Institutional Ethics Committee (IECs) in India following guidelines for research on Human Participants as laid down by the Indian Council of Medical research (ICMR), New Delhi.

The **National Research Act** in 1974 created the National Commission for the protection of Human Subjects in Biomedical and Behavioural Research (National Research Act. 1974) with the purpose to identify the basic ethical principles that needs to be followed during biomedical and behavioural research which involve human participants, and thereby, to formulate necessary guidelines to be followed in order to ensure such research is conducted in accordance with those principles. The National Commission took the charge and prepared the **Belmont Report** in 1979. The Belmont Report is a statement of basic guidelines that provide "an analytical framework to guide the resolution of the ethical problems arising from research with human subjects". The Belmont Report was presented in three topics of discussion which include: boundaries between practice and research, basic ethical principles, and applications (Belmont Report Vol. I & II 1979). It consists of three basic principles:

1. **Respect for Persons**
   - ❖ Initial and continuing review of research
   - ❖ Allow people to withdraw and treat them as autonomous agents (having the right to self-govern).
   - ❖ Maintain the welfare of subjects and protect those who have diminished autonomy (vulnerable populations) like children, prisoners, and elderly.

2. **Principle of Beneficence**
   - ❖ Social and scientific value to research. Do no harm.

GREATS - Guidelines for Research Ethics in Anthropological Studies   111

❖ Scientific validity to research. Not an act of kindness or charity, but a concrete obligation.

❖ Favourable risk: benefit ratio.

3. **Principle of Justice**

❖ Fair subject selection/recruitment

❖ Appropriate inclusion and exclusion criteria

❖ Fair distribution of the risks and the benefits of research based upon the problem or issue under investigation

The three general principles in the conduct of research lead to the consideration of

✓ Informed Consent process

✓ Risk/Benefit assessment

✓ Selection of research participants

The Belmont Report thus treated as guidelines and a detailed statement of basic ethical principles that could assist in resolving the ethical problems which might arises while conducting research on human participants that surround while conducting research with human subjects.

In 1980 the Indian Council of Medical research (ICMR), New Delhi brought out for the first time in India, the 'Policy Statement on Ethical Considerations involved in Research on human Subjects'. It was followed by revised guidelines in 2000 named as the 'Ethical Guidelines for Biomedical Research on Human Subjects', which later renamed as 'Ethical Guidelines for Biomedical Research on Human Participants', and stated it as **ICMR Code** in 2006 (Indian Council of Medical Research 2006). In 1982 the Council for International Organizations of Medical Sciences (CIOMS) along with the World Health Organization (WHO) jointly issued the 'Proposed International guidelines for Biomedical Research involving

Human Subjects'. It was the CIOMS which subsequently brought out the 'International Guidelines for Ethical Review in Epidemiological Studies' in 1991 which was followed by 'International Ethical Guidelines for Biomedical Research involving Human Subjects'in 1993 (Indian Council of Medical Research 2006; WHO-CIOMS 2016). The guidelines as given in ICMR code stated 12 principles to be followed for any research using human beings as participants and should be treated as common to all areas of biomedical research (Indian Council of Medical Research 2006).

These are:

i. Principles of Essentiality

ii. Principles of voluntariness, informed consent and community agreement

iii. Principles of non-exploitation

iv. Principles of privacy and confidentiality

v. Principles of precaution and risk minimization

vi. Principles of professional competence

vii. Principles of accountability and transparency

viii. Principles of maximization of the public interest as well as of distributive justice

ix. Principles of Institutional arrangements

x. Principles of public domain

xi. Principles of totality and responsibility, and

xii. Principles of compliance

Bill Dutton (2010) highlighted six key principles of Research in Social Sciences which include -

1. Research should be designed, reviewed and undertaken in such a way that it must ensure integrity, quality and transparency.

GREATS - *Guidelines for Research Ethics in Anthropological Studies* 113

2. Research staff and participants must be informed fully about the purpose of the study, the methods and possible uses of the research intended including what their participation in the research entails as well as what kind of risks involved, if any whatsoever.

3. The confidentiality of information shared by the research participants and the anonymity of respondents should be respected.

4. Research participants must therefore take part voluntarily, whole-heartedly, free will, and free from any coercion, whatsoever and howsoever.

5. It is the responsibility of the researcher(s) to avoid any instances causing harm to research participants, in strict sense.

6. The independence of research should be clear and must be explicit from any kind of conflicts of interest or partiality.

In addition to the above mentioned points, the report highlights key procedural issues for implementing these principles (Dutton 2010)-

(a) The responsibility for conducting a research in line with relevant principles solely rests upon the principal investigator and the concerned research / employing organization.

(b) The responsibility for ensuring that research is subject to appropriate ethics review, approval and monitoring lies with the research organization seeking or holding an award…and which employs the researchers performing it, or some of the researchers when it is acting as the coordinator for collaborative research involving more than one organization.

(c) Research organizations must have clear, transparent, appropriate and effective procedures in place for ethics review, approval and governance whenever it is necessary.

(d) To ensure that the risks should be minimized.

(e) Research should be designed in a way that the dignity and autonomy of research participants is protected and respected at all times.

(f) Ethics review should always be proportionate to the potential risk it is associated with whether the study involves primary data or any secondary data.

(g) Usually the secondary use of some datasets could be uncontroversial in relative sense, and might require little touch of ethical review. However, the novel use of existing data and especially data linkage, as well as some uses of administrative and secure data will raise issues of ethics.

(h) Unlike secondary data research, the research involving primary data collection would always raise issues of ethics that therefore must be addressed clearly.

In 2018 the European Commission postulated **Ethics in Social Science and Humanities** in a much detailed way[11]. It is clearly mentioned that by acknowledging their responsibilities, social scientists help build and maintain the trust of various social groupings – whether research participants, collaborators, members of the public, or funding bodies – that is necessary to conduct social science research in the first place. Social scientists commonly face ethical problems, and although ethics can be considered an everyday aspect of research practice, they are becoming more complex. Social Sciences research is dynamic, progressive and developmental, raising new issues and concerns as new foci for research evolve and new ways to collect and analyze data become possible. There is a need for ethically sensitive decisions at all stages of the research process. As a researcher, you are therefore encouraged to engage in continued reflection on any new ethical concerns that emerge while performing your work and on their potential implications for your own work, your research participants, communities and society in general. Moreover, you are encouraged to document and share such concerns within your project and your community of researchers (Ethics in Social Science and Humanities 2019).

By following all the guidelines available (both national and international) it was found that Ethical Guidelines for conducting research in Anthropological and Allied Sciences is desperately needed and therefore, must have an Institutional Ethics Committee (IEC) for monitoring and governing the ethical issues related to research in Social Science and Humanities, including Anthropology. An appraisal for **GREATS** – Guidelines for Ethical Research in Anthropological Studies is given below for consideration to postulate guidelines and proposal for IEC in Social Sciences Research in India.

GREATS: GUIDELINES FOR RESEARCH ETHICS IN ANTHROPOLOGICAL STUDIES

Ethical Issues in Anthropological Research: An Appraisal towards the need of an Institutional Ethics Committee for research on Human Subjects in Anthropological & Allied Sciences.

GREATS: An Appraisal

1. To design and implement research in accordance with the IEC along with the principles as given in various reports like Belmont, ICMR etc.

   ❖ Responsibility as an investigator is to design and implement the study in accord with the ethical principles.

   ❖ Scientific justification of the study, and its significance must be clearly stated which include the needs of the population(s), and at large the state/country, in which the research is carried out. Furthermore it encompasses the investigators' views of the issues and considerations rose by the study regarding ethics, that how properly it is mentioned, and how the proposed is dealt with them.

2. Protection of Human Participants / Key Cultural Consultants

   ❖ The IEC must have an Office of Human Research Protection which will keep proper documentation / agreement that the Institution has through the Department involved says this is how we are going to protect human subjects.

   ❖ The potential harm associated with participation in social science research is multifaceted. Addressing such harm appropriately requires care. Participants in social science studies are seldom exposed to physical harm, although they may sometimes experience transient psychological discomfort or even harm as a result activity itself.

   ❖ Risks can be non-material, including participant's personal values and beliefs, privacy, social standing, their links to family, their position within occupational settings, and the wider community. This may cause harm of various kinds: emotional, psychological, economic, reputational etc.

❖ Research ethics issues in social sciences are diverse and often very complex. The risks associated are also varied and therefore need to b systematically addressed according to the research ethics associated with each project. The responsibilities incumbent on the research teams to identify and prevent potential harm can be significant.

3. **Obtaining prior IEC approval**

❖ Insure that all research involving human subjects is submitted and approved by the appropriate IEC prior to the actual commencement of the study. Make sure activities that should fall under the Research Ethics are brought to the IEC before they are implemented.

❖ The purpose of submitting proposals to IEC is not only confined to determine whether they qualify for ethical review but also to assess their ethical acceptability.

4. **Complying with the IEC Requirements**

❖ It includes policies, procedures, and decision. Investigators are responsible for following IEC guidelines, policies, procedures, conditions, and decisions. The study will be under the IEC scanner through different types of review which include: Initial review, continuation review, amendment reviews, non-compliance review, and expedited or full review. Privacy and confidentiality towards respect for participants will be under continuous monitoring through reviews.

118   *Research Ethics, Indigenous Communities and Fieldwork*

5. **Implementing the protocol as Approved**

    ❖ Implement the research as approved and obtained prior IEC approval of modification. Do not change without prior IEC approval. Modifications/ Amendments need prior IEC approval to implement to ensure compliance.

6. **Obtaining Informed Consent/Assent**

    ❖ In accordance with the regulations as approved by the IEC. One may follow the ICMR guidelines.

    ❖ Give participants a clear explanation of the overall purpose, aims, methods and implications of the research.

    ❖ The voluntary consent of the human participant is absolutely essential. Explain that the participation is voluntary and there is no pressure whatsoever from the researcher's end.

    ❖ Remind them that they have the right to withdraw their consent at any time without any consequences.

    ❖ Explain the degree of benefit, risks, burden or discomfort involved in participation.

    ❖ Disclose who will benefit form the research.

    ❖ Give a firm commitment to protecting respondents' anonymity and privacy.

7. **Documentation of Informed Consent/Assent.**

    ❖ Proper documentation of the consent forms. One must have written consent. Telephonic / verbal consent and likewise modes are not to be entertained. The investigator should have the patience to obtain the written consent from the participants. Must date and sign the form. Provide subject with a copy and maintain the documentation. If needed keep a scan copy of each consent as back up.

8. **Submitting Progress Reports within the stipulated time.**

   ❖ To submit the report in a timely manner. To submit adequate information to the IEC in order to seek approval for continuation. Investigator is not supposed to continue prior to the re-approval of the study.

9. **Reporting unanticipated problems to IEC.**

   ❖ Repot to IEC for any injuries, adverse effects or other unanticipated problems involving risk to participants or others. To find out IEC's policies and what needs to be reported. The investigator should know the different requirements for the particular study, and thereby follow further instructions as given by the IEC.

10. **Retaining Records, Data Protection, and Privacy.**

   ❖ It is the investigator's responsibility to retain signed consent, documents, IEC research records, schedules/questionnaires etc., for at least three years past completion of research activity. It also includes the research protocols, grant applications, grant documents, and all correspondences. It is however reasonable to mention that the researcher may keep the record for even longer time mainly if it is multi-centered study or a cohort study etc.

   ❖ The main task face by a participant in social sciences research is disclosure of identity and insufficient protection of their private information, associated with discrimination and stigmatization. Safeguarding privacy and appropriate measures for processing, handling, and storing data are thus central at all stages of research and beyond.

❖ Data protection is both an integral issue of research ethics and a fundamental human right. It is closely linked to human dignity and the principle that everyone should be values and respected. It must be rigorously applied by the research community.

11. Public Accountability for Research Outputs.

❖ For realizing the social and scientific value of research public accountability is of utmost necessity. Researchers must therefore have an obligation to comply with recognized publication ethics related to research outputs or results.

❖ Researchers should publish the results of all research analyses prospectively or otherwise be made available in the public domain.

❖ It should be mandatory for any publication or report resulting from a research that the investigators must mention the name of the Institutional Ethics Committee which has approved or authorized the study.

12. Conflict of Interest

❖ Sometime there arise conflicts between the primary purpose of the research and secondary interests which could influence one or more stages of the research. It could be choice of research hypothesis or questions and methods, regarding recruitment and retention of participants, conflict s arising in interpretation and publication of data, and so does the ethical review of the on-going research.

GREATS - Guidelines for Research Ethics in Anthropological Studies   121

❖ It is therefore reasonable to mention that it is necessary to develop and implement policies and procedures to identify, mitigate, and eliminate such problems on one hand, or else manage such conflicts of interest on the other hand.

❖ It is the duty of the researchers that they must disclose conflicts of interest, if raised, on their part to the institutional ethics committees designated in order to evaluate and manage such conflicts.

Requirements for Establishing Institutional Ethics Committee

❖ For undergraduate and post graduate studies, the department concerned may have Standard Operating Procedures (SOPs) to conduct field work as per the curriculum of the Institute / University. The head of the department, in this case, could handle and monitor the process.

❖ For M.Phil., Ph.D., and thereafter any Professional or Sponsored field works must be routed through the Institutional Ethics Committee (IEC) following **GREATS**.

❖ The IEC must be constituted according to a document that clearly specifies the manner in which the members and the chair will be appointed, replaced, and reappointed. The IEC must be formed in such a way that the members are competent enough for providing bias-free and thorough review of research proposals, and must include members representing indigenous groups. It is desirable that there will be regular rotation of members in order to keep balance between both the advantages of experience of senior personnel to that of junior faculty.

122 *Research Ethics, Indigenous Communities and Fieldwork*

❖ When a research proposal involves vulnerable groups or individuals, such protocols must be reviewed with prior consent from the representatives of relevant advocacy groups either by invitation or over telephone etc. If it is not feasible to invite then at least an informed consent from the relevant groups should be obtained prior to IEC approval.

❖ The members of the IEC must update their knowledge about the ethical conduct of research at regular interval. In case if the committee doesn't have the relevant expertise to review a protocol adequately, there must be some provision through which they could consult with external persons having adequate skills or certified authority. Committees must keep the records of their deliberations and decisions.

❖ The formation of IEC, its members, and duration must be informed or updated to the Indian Council of Social Sciences Research, New Delhi, time to time.

Acknowledgement

The Institutional Review Board of the University of Alabama at Birmingham, Alabama, USA where I've been a visiting scientist during 2014-15 and learned a lot about the guidelines related to ethical issues to do research on human subjects.

References

Merriam-Webster. https://www.merriam-webster.com/dictionary/ethic accessed on 02/05/2020

World health Organization. Ethical standards and procedures for research with human beings. https://www.who.int/ethics/research/en/ accessed on 02/05/2020.

Nuremberg Code 1947. "Trials of War Criminals before the Nuremberg Military Tribunals under Control Council Law No.

GREATS - Guidelines for Research Ethics in Anthropological Studies   123

10", Vol. 2, pp. 181-182. Washington, D.C.: U.S. Government Printing Office, 1949. https://history.nih.gov/research/downloads/nuremberg.pdf accessed on 02/05/2020.

Declaration of Helsinki. 1964. Ethical Principles for Medical Research Involving Human Subjects. Bulletin of the World Health Organization, 2001; 79: 373-374. https://www.who.int/bulletin/archives/79(4)373.pdf accessed on 02/05/2020.

National Research Act. 1974. https://history.nih.gov/research/downloads/PL93-348.pdf accessed on 06/05/2020.

Belmont Report (Vol. I). 1979. https://videocast.nih.gov/pdf/ohrp_appendix_belmont_report_vol_1.pdf accessed on 02/05/2020.

Belmont Report (Vol. II). 1979. https://videocast.nih.gov/pdf/ohrp_appendix_belmont_report_vol_2.pdf accessed on 02/05/2020.

Indian Council of Medical Research (ICMR). 2006. Ethical Guidelines for Biomedical Research on Human Participants. ICMR, New Delhi.

http://www.cns.iisc.ac.in/wordpress/wp-content/uploads/2017/01/ethical_guidelines.pdf accessed on 05/02/2020.

WHO-CIOMS. 2016. International Ethical Guidelines for Health-related Research Involving Humans. https://cioms.ch/wp-content/uploads/2017/01/WEB-CIOMS-EthicalGuidelines.pdf accessed on 06/02/2020.

Dutton B. 2010. Six Principles to Guide Research Ethics in the Social Sciences. https://billdutton.me/2010/02/05/principles-to-guide-research-ethics-in-the-social-sciences/ accessed on 02/05/2020.

Ethics in Social Science and Humanities. 2019. European Commission. https://ec.europa.eu/research/participants/data/ref/h2020/other /hi/ h2020_ethics-soc-science-humanities_en.pdf accessed on 02/05/2020.